RAISING STRONG DAUGHTERS

RAISING STRONG DAUGHTERS

JEANETTE GADEBERG

FAIRVIEW PRESS   *Minneapolis*

Published by Fairview Press, 2450 Riverside Avenue, Minneapolis MN 55454.

Fairview Press is a division of Fairview Health Services, a community-focused health system, affiliated with the University of Minnesota, providing a complete range of services, from the prevention of illness and injury to care for the most complex medical conditions. For a free current catalog of Fairview Press titles, call toll-free 1-800-544-8207, or visit our Web site at www.fairviewpress.org.

Excerpt from *A Message* by Bobbi Linkletter on page 22 (copyright © 1993) is printed by permission of the author.

ISBN–10: 0-925190-98-5
ISBN–13: 978-0-925190-98-7

Library of Congress Cataloging-in-Publication Data
Gadeberg, Jeanette, 1953–
        Raising strong daughters / Jeanette Gadeberg.
                p. cm.
        ISBN 0-925190-98-5 : $12.95
        1. Mothers and daughters.   2. Parenting.   I. Title.
        HQ755.85.G3   1995
        649'.133—dc20   95-3893
                                                             CIP

First printing: April 1995
First paperback printing: May 1996

Printed in the United States of America
10 09 08 07 06 05   11 10 9 8 7 6

Cover design: Circus Design

To the girls and women in my family

With love to my mother—
Edna Marian Gadeberg
who has always been there for me,
loving and supporting me and telling me I could do it

And to my extraordinary daughters whom I dearly love—
Rosemary Park Shultz
whose gentle spirit melts hearts
and
Mariel Kim Shultz,
whose smile lights up the room

Also
Marian Elizabeth Nelson
my creative and very Scandinavian sister
and
Elaine Marian Nelson
my most dear niece

CONTENTS

ACKNOWLEDGMENTS

A warm and heartfelt thank you to all my friends and family who have been there for me during this exhilarating process. Many of these people and I go back many years; they were ever present and supportive during my own time of personal change and growth. They have understood and they have cared. I won't forget.

More specifically, great love and thanks to my mother, Edna Gadeberg, who has always been there for me telling me I could do it. You support, love, and do all the everyday helpful things that have kept my daughters' and my life on track these past few years. Your bountiful day-to-day support and care made it possible for me to have the time and energy to complete this book.

And thank you to my daughters, Rosemary and Mariel—my smart, funny, loving, and extraordinary girls. I love you more than life itself.

And to Susan Walker who is my dear friend exceptionale, my confidante, and like another mother to my girls. Your presence in my life continually brings me great joy and inspires me toward excellence, education, the arts, and an abundant and full life. You have enriched my life in countless ways with your unfailing generosity, love of books, and sense of humor. You are truly the best of friends.

To Becky Danielson, teacher, friend, brand new mother, one of the first readers of my material, and my daughter Rosemary's kindergarten and first grade teacher: Thank you for sticking with us, offering friendship, fresh herbs, great food, and a gentle touch. And thank you for providing my daughter with quintessentially perfect school years by sharing your magic, your talent, and your love with my little girl for her very first years of school. Through your creativity you made it clear that the kindergarten moment was happening and all was well with the world. In that special place called kindergarten, enchantment still lives! Neither one of us has ever forgotten kindergarten or you.

To Beth Halbrook for your glorious sense of humor and your generous gifts of time, energy, and friendship: You are always there for me and my daughters.

To Greg Ohland, a special and wonderful man who knows what really matters in life: Thank you for your support and encouragement and for adding an extra measure of fun and joy to my life.

To Dan Nelson, my brother-in-law: You have been an excellent and dedicated father to my niece, raising her to be a strong, successful young woman.

To Joanne Burgio, Ph.D. whose professional camaraderie and friendship over many years is a treasure: "Listening with Your Eyes" was developed from an idea of yours. Many thanks!

To Tom Linzmeier, stockbroker and long time steady friend that I can count on: Thanks for helping me crunch the numbers.

To The Blake School: a particular thank you for the opportunities you provide and your achievement of excellence on behalf of my daughters.

And to my editor, Julie Odland, and the rest of the staff at Fairview Press: Thank you to Julie for your support and warmth and thank you to all of Fairview Press for listening and believing in me and my message!

YESTERDAY'S DAUGHTERS

In a world that has turned upside down from even twenty years ago, isn't it wonderful to know that we really can do something to help raise our daughters to become strong, confident, happy, independent women?

As adults, how do we respond to the growing tide of fear, confusion, and inequality the world often throws at our girls? How do we help our daughters develop the inner strength they need to be able to respond proactively and creatively to a world that at times is not user-friendly? We must face the glaring reality that part of the reason the world was easier in previous years was because of the rigid and narrow roles in which girls and women were imprisoned. Girls were taught to be nice, polite, and subservient. Women were assigned kitchen duty, given an allowance, and directed by others.

We must acknowledge how frightening and conflicted the world itself has become. While we face a troubled world, we cannot bury our heads in the sand. Strangers hurt our children. The American Dream is not so readily attainable. Families struggle with several issues. Later on our girls will encounter a complex job market with increased competition. The list of difficulties our daughters may have to face can seem overwhelming. The issues of gender inequality are as powerful today as they were during the more pronounced times of the women's movement. We have no one-size-fits-all answer or directive for how women should live their lives. It is grossly unfair to women to suggest that all women should define their lives in the same way.

Startling statistics

It is true that the role and power of women have expanded greatly over the past decades. Women's voices are listened to in the marketplace, at home, and in the community. Consider, however, these current, disturbing statistics regarding girls and women:

- Women and girls are half the world's population and do two-thirds of the world's work, but receive one-tenth of the world's income and own less than a hundredth of the world's property.[1]
- In 1992 18,000 boys were eligible for National Merit Scholarships versus 8,000 girls.[2]
- In 1992 boys had higher scores than girls on eleven of fourteen subjects on the Scholastic Aptitude Test.[3]
- Worldwide 76 million fewer girls than boys receive schooling.[4]
- Female education, rather than wealth of a country influences its birth rate.[5]
- In school, boys are called on eight times more often than girls and in general receive more attention.[6]
- 9.9 million American women are currently divorced.[7]
- 11.2 million women have lost a spouse to death.[8]
- 12 million women are single heads-of-household.[9]

Why did I write *Raising Strong Daughters?* Because over the years that I have worked as a psychotherapist, I have watched countless adult women come into counseling struggling with basic issues of low self-esteem, wavering self-identity, fears, and anxieties. They have been fighting themselves and a less-than-supportive outside world. They have felt unable to claim their innate rights to state clearly their opinions and to make their own solid decisions and choices. Many have not known what their opinions and choices were. I have watched them grapple with new roles and responsibilities for which they were never prepared. It has been hard to see their hurt and confusion. Over time it became clear to me: what if we could back up with these women, back way up to when they were young girls—when they could have been taught what they needed to know to do this thing called life and do it in a way that was right for them?

Grown women are still struggling and grappling with old, broken-down familial and societal messages—messages that undermine their strength and their ability to forge ahead to create new destinies that include rock-solid self-esteem, confidence, and assertiveness. These messages were woven into their younger years and carried forward into adulthood. Now they are mixed in with today's often confusing messages and debates about what women's lives should be. Today's women are expected to listen and adhere to the polarizing and conflicting messages they hear. Women are expected to define their lives in opposing opposites depending on which group is doing the talking. One group expects them to be pro-choice, another pro-life. They are pressured to work outside the home in a full-blown career yet also to stay home and mother their children full-time. Some expect them to identify themselves as feminists, others snub this term as "too radical." Women can't win. They have gone from the narrow, rigid role-definition of the earlier decades to the demands of being all things to all people. The bottom line is that today's women find themselves in the same historical quandary of yesteryear, just with different scenery. Women's lives are still being directed by a grand scheme masterminded by others. They are managed by many rather than trained from an early age to listen to their own inner voice.

It is easy to get lulled into thinking that the lives of women are at a satisfactory standpoint. After all, they are free to work outside the home, earn and handle their own money, own property, vote, end an unwanted pregnancy, live singly, or start a business. Yet, just twenty years ago when applying for a home mortgage, a married woman's full-time income was reduced to 1/3 of the actual dollar amount simply because she was a woman and might get pregnant. Never mind that she had a college degree and worked full-time. She apparently was considered to be unable to control her pregnancies. This same twenty years ago found many women mandated to wear dresses to work. Slacks were not allowed on women in many places of business. Twenty-five years ago, girls had to wear dresses to public schools. They were thrilled and excited to have "pants day" once a year. Girls and women had to wait for permission to dress as they wished and to have their money counted dollar for dollar with a man's.

Many of the women who experienced these ridiculous inequities are now today's mothers. These women who grew up with confounding messages are now struggling to sort out the "new freedoms" for themselves and their daughters. Unfortunately, many groups continue to behave as though their truth is the only truth. Women are still left in the position of listening to the voices and demands of others.

Archaic messages alive and well

In an effort to sort out how women have arrived at where and who they are today and to provide a foundation from which to move forward with today's daughters, it behooves us to revisit a few of the messages that have been deeply embedded in the minds and belief systems of many of today's women. As a reader, reflect on your own experiences growing up, or those of the women in your life. Consider the impact the messages have had on you whether you're a woman or a man and how you in turn are raising your daughter.

"What more do you want?"

This message implies that women are asking for far more than they have a right to—that women already have enough. This tells women their dissatisfaction is their own problem and stems from a low-level greed. It defines femininity as quiet, uncomplaining satisfaction. It curtails the dreams and aspirations of women and keeps them confined in small and safe lives. Ultimately, it keeps them dependent on someone else to provide a life and livelihood for them.

"Women's income is secondary"

Many single mothers quickly come to the conclusion that what they really need is a wife. Married women often find that it's actually easier to complete all the home tasks themselves rather than play the nagging/waiting game. Too many women come home from a full day working outside the home to a full-time homemaker/mother job. The husband of a woman I know insists that she skip her own lunch hour to come home and make his lunch and visit with him. He gets mad if she doesn't. Times have not changed much. Women are mothers, homemakers, and workers outside the home. Who says women are the weaker sex?

Women's income has long been a topic of discussion. At least women working outside the home are no longer viewed as simply earning "pin-money" or "egg money." They are, however, frequently confined to narrow fields that are best known for their low wages, poor benefits, and inflexibility. Today's working women often were not trained from an early age to undertake the tougher subjects at school to prepare for greater professional responsibilities and goals. They missed opportunities for mentorships, coaches, and competitions. They grew to be women qualified only for lower-level positions. Their income is still often seen as merely supplementary and expendable. If they complain about anything at work, they are told by spouses and others to simply quit their jobs. Rather than acknowledge their work as vital, important, and worth the effort to effectively problem-solve, they are encouraged to give up and walk away.

This lack of preparation—both academically and internally—leads to the mass of women whose feet are stuck to the floor of the pink collar ghetto, with low-paying, low-power jobs that don't go anywhere and never allow women to get ahead or to soar. Their wings are clipped. These jobs require women to become mindless order-takers; the jobs rarely offer an ounce of job or career security. The fortunate women who were prepared and trained for reality fare decidedly better. They have degrees, more dollars, and greater autonomy. They also tend to bang their heads on the glass ceiling in their attempt to get up and out of the trenches. Perhaps only women entrepreneurs have the most promising opportunities for true freedom, power, and financial security. We must train our daughters to be pioneers, for their own safety and satisfaction.

"Keep your voice down; be polite"

This message admonishes women not to embarrass anyone with their loud, strident voices or opinions. They are told "just don't say anything, let it go, leave it alone." It doesn't matter whether their feelings are hurt or upset, they'll get over it. Being outspoken is considered an unattractive feature in a woman. Strong, successful, and powerful women are advised to "soften" their image. Articulate, intelligent, outspoken, and opinionated women are called derogatory names. Men with similar traits are hailed as leaders; women are told they have an "image problem."

Women of today are held at bay by old messages urging them to remain softly in the shadows. Currently women are allowed by society to have opinions as long as their opinions are fairly mainstream. I work with many female clients who feel unable to voice their opinions or expectations to their partners for fear of "hurting his feelings" or appearing too demanding. They are also afraid they wouldn't be listened to. Some are made to feel that their comments and conversation are unimportant. Many are accused of "going on and on" about their worries and concerns, which are seen as being nagging and boring. Perhaps their concerns and worries would be lessened if they were listened to and taken seriously. Many are afraid if they demand too much they will be left.

"Math is tough"

This statement came via Mattel's Barbie doll. It was pulled from the market following the outcry of intelligent women. Many of today's adult women were not urged to attend college or pursue the hard sciences. Therefore, many are not facile in today's high-tech work environment. Computers remain frightening and foreign to many adult women. The reality is that the 1990's is the age of the electronic superhighway. If women are not plugged into it, they are missing a lot! No one need be a slave to the media, the television, or the computer-driven business world, but when women are uncomfortable around the main source of information-processing they are put at a distinct and crucial disadvantage. During their school years they often brushed by or virtually ignored foreign language, physics, chemistry, and advanced math. They got the message that they were to bypass the hard, tough academic classes. In fact, most adult women over the age of thirty were required to take home economics and sewing in school. There is nothing wrong with these subjects; the problem is that girls were required to pursue only one path designated specifically for females. They were not supported to take the math and sciences route. Many girls were told they wouldn't be able to do it. This hardly engenders the confidence required to dig in and excel. With this hole in their basic education, today's adult working women are often limited by their lack of skill and experience in this vital area. They find it next-to-impossible to move ahead into the upper echelons of their careers. And thus one of the great divisions results between men and women in the marketplace. We are back to the problem of glass ceilings, sticky floors, and pink collar ghettos. Women are held back by the gaps and neglect they experienced thirty, forty, and fifty years ago.

The deficiencies, however, go well beyond computers to include most mechanical or analytical subjects. Girls aspired to enter the softer fields and were guided toward courses that ill prepared them for competitive careers. Today's girls cannot be left with mushy, go-nowhere academic backgrounds. They must pursue the difficult.

"It's OK to hit women"

Most readers will disagree with the above statement. Most don't believe this is OK nor do they condone violence; they personally don't know men who abuse women. Yet society is overflowing with violence. Women are potentially under attack from every corner. The entertainment industry both subliminally and overtly condones and even promotes violence against women. Rare is the movie that does not slip in at least a subtle, titillating scene of a women being frightened, stalked, terrorized, abused, and even murdered by a partner or stranger. Video games are burgeoning with violence. Male sports and media superheroes are idolized as hale and hearty folk legends even after being exposed as wife-beaters.

The message of violence is grounded in families and society that say men are more important than women. Men are portrayed as physically strong but unable to control their behaviors and actions. Women are blamed for provoking outrageous behavior from men. Society often overlooks the personal responsibility of men. Girls and women tolerate abuse and return again and again for more, each time forgiving their abusers. They don't leave for a myriad of reasons: they are afraid, they are dependent, they know the statistics that indicate that when women decide to leave they have the greatest chance of being murdered by their abuser; many refuse to leave for fear of "hurting his feelings." Women who stay mistily report that when things are going well, he is loving, considerate and "his real self." They are willing to wait out the violence, convinced if they would just do everything right and as he asks, he won't hit again. Some don't live to see this happen.

"Be thin; be beautiful"

Women's bodies are poked, evaluated, judged, and surveyed by a vast array of other people. Today's women grew up in a time of rigidly defined ideas of how girls and women should dress and wear their hair. Today they face the added hype of the demand for the ultimate in-shape body. Being physically fit is in fact a healthy, worthwhile choice, but why can't women's bodies simply be their own? Why must decisions on how they look and how they are shaped belong to someone else: media, men, other women, or diet and exercise programs? Women's body shape is no one's business but their own. Unfortunately, even individual women are hard-pressed to appreciate their own bodies. They are brainwashed by pictures, messages, demands, expectations, and judgments that tell them that the women they see pictured in the media are normal, but they are not. Any sense of self-confidence and esteem is shattered when they compare themselves in the mirror to these toothpicks in the media—thin young women wearing sensational outfits who have been professionally made-up to look natural. Real women over age twenty typically carry a few extra pounds and have lines and wrinkles that acknowledge a genuine life replete with laughter and tears. They may have a less-than-perfect haircut. They may only have time in the morning to slap a minor dollop of makeup (if that) on before heading out of the house for a full-speed day. These real women are reduced to feeling shame when they see their reflections. These are honest women who do their best to make ends meet, fulfill enormous responsibilities, and manage to laugh and love along the way. Real women need real clothes for realistic bodies, plus a society that honors and respects them for their valiant efforts and successes at living full-time real lives!

"You need a man"

Women get the message that being in a relationship with a man, even if it's bad, is better than not having a man at all—being alone. This dependency on men and relationships is common among girls and women. Having a boyfriend or a man becomes so important that women may overlook the poor quality of the relationship just to be able to feel they are connected to someone. This need for connectedness is the pull that draws us all into relationships. Most people, men and women, want someone to come home to at the end of the day, to have someone truly "be there" to share life. This rather glorious need of ours to be in a relationship can be pure nectar, sweetening our lives and giving us purpose and energy. But for girls and women, the snag is based in the fear of being alone in the world. They feel they need to be close to someone, anyone, as opposed to being alone. Being alone gets twisted with the fear of loneliness. In fact, the two are quite different. Girls and women receive the message subtly and overtly that they really can't do it on their own. This thing called life is presented to them as being too big, too complicated, too much responsibility. At an early age a deep unsettling and undermining fear is instilled within their very souls. And so they settle for any man or boy who will have them just so they don't have be alone.

"You must have children to be complete and fulfilled as a woman"

Can we bravely give our daughters the message that they do not have to have children should they choose not to? This is a decidedly difficult message for most people to consider. Many see raising children—a family—as the ultimate fulfillment, a life of supreme joys and heart-stopping sorrows worth every minute. Years ago, this was the only path for a woman to follow. Our daughters will not have to pursue a life filled with children should they choose not to. Can we graciously allow our daughters this choice?

"Act like a lady"

The term *lady* usually translates into an unrealistic rendition of an unassertive woman lacking in confidence, personal power, and esteem. Nothing is wrong with the term *lady*. Rather, the issue is about the implication that real women shouldn't be strong-minded, independent, or rock solid. We must teach girls to be fair and flexible but never to be door mats. The characteristics often ascribed to "ladies" are gentility, good manners, and sweet dispositions. These features are not bad; we simply need to make certain today's girls are steeped in self-confidence and know-how. Thirty years ago teenage girls used to attend programs such as "Glamorama" where they received hat boxes filled with beauty aides and learned to walk and sit correctly, listen to fashion, make-up and hair tips, and learn general "ladylike" protocol. Junior high school home economics classes taught girls how to get in and out of cars demurely, to plan balanced meals for future families, and to measure bodies for proper sewing pattern fit. Girls felt shame as they had to line up in the front of classrooms to show the difference in body types (read development and weight) and pattern sizes. Ugh! Today everything girls learn needs to be taught in the context of the realistic demands of tomorrow. Real women can be ladies, but real women must also be confident, independent and strong!

"Don't be angry"

Anger is a tough and complex issue that is part of being human. Women used to be taught to subdue any anger they felt. Books and movies depicting foregone eras portray young women having to bury their heads in pillows to release their anger without being heard. Women were to shed tears only while running the water in the bathroom sink (this technique is still used by many). Heart-pounding, intense feelings were to be buried rather than dealt with and resolved. Many women still do not have the basic skills needed to express their feelings constructively, particularly feelings of anger. Society more readily accepts sadness and tears as women's proper response to anger. Perhaps this is part of the reason a large number of women are depressed; depression is a socially acceptable diagnosis for women's inner pain and struggle.

Adult women may have to address their own issues of anger and frustration to show their daughters the way toward emotional strength and health—to keep anger in perspective and not let it become an overwhelming force that has no proactive channel. Why are today's women angry? The reasons are as varied as the women themselves. Anger is good when it is channeled constructively. Why shouldn't women be upset in the face of injustice?

Unspoken messages

Perhaps the most powerful of all messages are the ones that were

11

never spoken, but by which a family unquestioningly lives. These unspoken words rule lives. Perhaps it is their very wordlessness that makes them so powerful. The results of these rules can be seen in daily behavior, by decisions made and values honored. These unspoken rules can be about money, the role of women, education, or the values of the family. The rules are played out in interactions between family members as well as between the family and society. What attitudes and beliefs are accepted and which are shunned? What behaviors are tolerated and which ones squelched?

These unspoken rules often affect girls and women. Are women respected or dismissed? How are successful women referred to? How are women spoken to within the family? What are the expectations for girls and women, especially in relation to men and work (both at home and in businesses)? These unspoken rules are reinforced by tradition; to question them shifts the balance of power within the family. We need to challenge old messages so we can find the courage as families and as a society to embrace "freedom and justice for all."

Today's girls, tomorrow's women

You have seen a few of the messages against which women of today struggle. Today's women probably can recollect many more from their own pasts. We must work hard to make certain we do not foist such destructive, undermining messages upon today's daughters. Let us move forward with today's girls to give them a deep sense of self-identity and inner strength. Today's girls will be facing a highly competitive, complex world where they will be required to make clear-headed choices for what is right for them and their families. Let us as today's adults show them how to develop the inner strength and resiliency that will allow them to walk boldly forward to an extraordinary future.

Strong girls—	Powerless girls—
1. let their voices ring out loud, clear, and strong.	1. are wishy-washy; they don't stand up for themselves.
2. are comfortable in and appreciate their bodies and their vitality.	2. are critical of their bodies.
3. actively and energetically participate in their world. They connect with positive people.	3. hide in the shadows and get lost in the crowd.
4. negotiate with ease.	4. run from conflict.
5. acknowledge, understand, and articulate their own value.	5. fade fast from low self-esteem.
6. are moving toward strong financial independence.	6. have no financial power.
7. have lives crackling with possibilities; they plan for success.	7. stay confused and unfocused about their futures.
8. rise up to pursue excellence and the challenges of lifelong learning.	8. shrink from the challenges of learning.
9. feel good from the inside and feel great about themselves.	9. lack confidence and gutsiness.
10. honor *her*story and personal identity.	10. struggle with wavering self-identity.

Notes

1. *United Nations World Conference Report.*

2. Quote: Elizabeth Kennan, President of Mount Holyoke College as cited in the Minneapolis-St. Paul *Star Tribune,* Feb. 14, 1994.

3. Sadner, Myra, and David Sadner *Failing At Fairness: How America's Schools Cheat Girls* New York: Scribner, 1994.

4. *Population Action International Study,* a Washington, D.C. based non-profit group as cited in Minneapolis-St. Paul *Star Tribune* Feb. 1, 1994. "The more educated women are, the likely they are to marry later, use birth control and have fewer, healthier children."

5. Ibid.

6. See note number 3 above.

7. Statistical Abstract of the United States 1994 (figures as of 1993) Table 59, Marital Status of the population by sex, race and Hispanic origin 1970-1993.

8. Ibid.

9. Figures for 1992. U.S. Department of Labor, Women's Bureau, *Facts on Working Women,* 93-3, June 1993.

RAISING AN OPINIONATED DAUGHTER

Society works slowly and subtly to stifle and silence girls. In school, boys have been routinely called on more often than girls to answer questions or perform. The media still tend to portray teenage girls as skinny creatures who crave the attention of boys. By the time they reach adolescence many girls would rather crawl into a hole than be the center of attention; many no longer want to be viewed as smart. For many, to be accepted and liked becomes a priority of such magnitude that they can't be themselves. Girls begin to prefer being overlooked and in the shadows, never causing anyone a moment's consternation. Some girls even begin to tolerate abuse, just for the opportunity to be what they think is "loved."

Learning to be opinionated and to stand up for herself and what she believes can help keep your daughter safe and increase her self-confidence. You can help her by showing her where and how to find a niche where she can express herself freely.

Helping your daughter learn to establish and voice her opinions will be hard work. When you challenge her to be willing to make noise and get noticed you may meet with some hefty resistance. The more training, nurturing and support she can receive at an early age the better her chances of becoming and remaining assertive. The

15

natural-born confidence of many girls tends to fade fast when they reach around ages twelve or thirteen. As a result, she could end up wasting her good talents and energy by disappearing into the woodwork for eight to ten years before rediscovering herself at age twenty or even age sixty. The goal is to prevent the great fade-out, which is a lot less work than having to help her reinvent her self-esteem and confidence later on. For many women, the search for self-worth unfortunately is a lifetime struggle. Do what you can now, at your daughter's early age to help her become comfortable enough with herself to venture into the risky world of self-expression.

When you challenge your daughter to give voice to her opinions it can be potentially embarrassing to you as a parent. Your daughter may give voice to opinions and statements that are not "politically correct" or even particularly disciplined at the time. Parents can heartily congratulate honest ventures into self-expression while they help a girl continue learning the process of how to express herself. When the going gets rough and the pressure is on, help her to figure out what she believes in. She does not have a wealth of experience and wisdom to draw on as she begins to stake out her territory. Learning to present her ideas to the world is a crucial cornerstone to her learning how to be heard throughout her life. She needs to be heard as an adult, in her career, in her relationships, and for herself. If she is allowed to slip quietly through life she will fade away and lose herself. The goal is to give her many opportunities to hear her own voice ring out loud, clear, and strong!

FRONT AND CENTER

Teaching your daughter to be brave, assertive, and involved requires a few basic tools and techniques. If she is naturally shy and quiet-spoken she may resist your attempts to nudge her into the limelight. The point is not to change her personality style, but to coach her in basic skills that augment her learning process.

Teach your daughter to sit up in the front

Front and center are ideal places to sit! Encourage her to be seen, be present, be obvious! Speakers, teachers, and presenters tend to spot the people right up in front first. The girl who sits there will be seen and heard. She will also be more apt to pay attention herself, taking in the nuances of body language and the energy and main points of the presenter. This enhances her own understanding of the subject matter being discussed and heightens her interest, simply because she is paying close attention. The girl who is up front experiences a different level of inclusion and involvement from being physically close to where the action is taking place. Hiding out in the back leaves more room for wandering minds and inattentiveness. The girl who is up front gets called on! By being in front your daughter makes a statement of her interest and intent to learn. Presenters and teachers love an interested audience and will gravitate toward your daughter's comments, responses, and interest level. She won't miss a thing, will get herself noticed, and will have a front-row seat to her own learning process.

Ask her how many times she raised her hand today to offer her input or answer a question

Encourage her to think things through, but be ready to throw in her two cent's worth. Teach her—unfailingly—that her opinions count, her thoughts are important, and her ideas are worthy of presentation and exploration. Urge her to volunteer for projects, to write answers on the board, to venture a guess, and to stand in front of the class and present. Spur her on to take risks and be the first one to try. Being bold may not come naturally to her. When you are together and you need a piece of information or require directions, role model for her how to request or give information. Be specific—every day, every week. Ask her when she jumped in to today's discussion. In which subjects does she seem more confident; from which ones does she shy away? Often girls feel less confident in

17

previously male-dominated subjects. If she seems especially unsure of herself in a particular area such as physical education, math, drama—whatever—this is a strong hint that she may need an extra boost of confidence-building experience. She may need to take an extra class after school, get some tutoring, or do some solution-focused problem solving with you to figure out how to solidify her skills.

Encourage her to sign up for classes that are traditionally boy-dominated subjects

She no longer has to "take on the school" to include herself in subjects predominantly taken by boys. Nor does she have to pretend to be interested in subjects that she is not. Expose your daughter to a wide variety of subject matter. This allows her to develop a true sense of what she likes and is interested in; it doesn't restrict her choices to the narrow path that the masses plod down. The well-worn path that everyone else takes may be just fine, but it may not be very creative and can actually be excruciatingly boring. For example, perhaps your daughter could excel in auto mechanics. Even if she doesn't thrill to the sound of a well-tuned motor, at least she would learn firsthand how her car engine (present or future) operates, when and what repairs are needed, and best of all—preventive maintenance. By taking one or two different, "masculine" class offerings, she can learn to handle basic machinery and tools. Parents and daughters can even sign up for auto or shop classes together through community education.

Prompt others to spotlight the girls

Have you ever noticed how often girls are left out of media coverage even when they were right there? When the media or school photographer arrives on the scene to photograph the participants in contests, scholarship programs, or school events, be aware! Watch the papers and news reports. Are the girls represented? If not, make noise—or better yet, encourage your daughter to make noise. Often a sizable number of the winners or participants are girls and yet not one single girl appears in the newspaper photo. Parents really have to pay attention to these things. It may seem trite and trivial, but it's not! It all adds together to the overt as well as subliminal message that boys are noticed and girls are simply left out—left out of pictures, articles, and other points of recognition. As a parent, continue to educate the media that girls exist and do wonderful things. And continue to embolden your daughter to announce her presence.

Urge your daughter to jump in with a topic for discussion

Encourage her at school, at dinner, at any event, to bring up topics of interest that she just read or learned about. Show her how to inspire herself and others to take an active interest in something she is learning. As she absorbs fascinating or disquieting facts about the world, help her to bring up these issues and get the conversation going. Does she read the newspaper? Whether she is in the first grade or high school, she can find articles worth bringing to school. Many schools have current events built into the week. If not, have your daughter suggest to her teacher that the class have a ten minute period each week where kids bring in news articles for discussion. Perhaps your daughter could start her own current events theme, collecting information pertaining to the experiences of girls and women. She could have her own information file to use throughout the school year or donate to the class or school library. Whenever your daughter is able to propose and implement a solid, workable plan, she is developing lifelong learning skills!

DISCUSS CONTROVERSIAL SUBJECTS

Here is something to liven up your dinner conversations: Engage your daughter in conversations and discussions about controversial subjects. Be willing to be quiet and listen to what she has to say. Pick her brain. Find out what she thinks. It may prove difficult to let her express opinions you find unacceptable because they are different from your own. It's easy to think theoretically that of course it is all right for your daughter to think and view the world differently than you do. Yet in reality, when she opens her mouth and says things so opposite of what you believe, it can be pretty hard to swallow. But doing so allows her to grow strong and independent and become a solid thinker in her own right.

Take a deep breath and start an honest, open-ended discussion about her viewpoints on abortion, date rape, sexual harassment, poverty, and money (for starters). This is not a time for you to preach your philosophy to her. Rather, it is an opportunity to find out what makes your daughter tick, to learn to understand how her reasoning works. Help her sort out her own thinking within the security of her family. This means you must provide a respectful forum for her to voice her opinions. Let your family be a safe place to have differing points of view. Give her a chance to roll up her sleeves and hammer out her values, sense of ethics, and citizenship. It's wonderful if you and your daughter can agree to disagree. This allows her to formulate her own thinking in a respectful conversation at home. Help her to think out loud so she can develop a strong, clear, solid sense of self-identity. You will be glad you did.

DEAR EDITOR

Submitting a letter to the editor and seeing her name and ideas in print can be pretty heady stuff for your daughter! Encourage her to respond to the issues of the day by putting words on her thoughts and feelings. She may be timid initially, but show her how to formulate the letter, where to send it, and where to watch for her letter in print. If she sends enough of them, over time one is bound to get printed. She can express her views on any topic that is on her mind or respond to a specific news event. She can submit letters to the editors of newspapers, magazines, newsletters, or television newscasts that solicit viewer response.

It is important that you not edit the letter for content. Try to control your urge to crawl into the woodwork if she writes something that in your opinion is outrageous. The goal is to encourage your daughter to speak her mind, the operative word being *her.* Of course, this can lead to rather embarrassing moments for you. You will have to be brave—simply wear a paper bag over your head for a few days until it all blows over. Seriously, your daughter will receive a powerful message regarding the worth of her opinion if you allow her to submit her written thoughts uncensored. Let her take personal responsibility for her opinion and live with the potential of conflict and disagreement. She will then have the opportunity to learn to live with her words and beliefs. She will learn to think through what she says and respond to criticism, challenge, and even verbal attack should someone vigorously respond to her letter with a differing point of view. What a great chance for her to learn the skills of creative dialogue.

Besides the rush of seeing her letter in print, it is also an opportunity for her to formulate her ideas about world issues. Her thinking will broaden as she considers all the facets of her topic. How does it affect her personally? What are the basic themes involved in the issue? Are other people being treated respectfully and given their personal freedom to live as they believe?

When is she old enough to submit a letter? Ignore age. It does not matter if she is six or sixteen. It does help, however, to add her age to her signature. Teach her to be proud of her youth and that young girls have good ideas and solid opinions. Teach her the importance of her signature on the letter. Forget the "anonymous" idea. Show her the value of speaking her mind and signing-off on her personal opinions. Let her experience the pride of a well-thought-out letter being presented to the rest of the city for review.

UPPITY GIRLS

A MESSAGE

I hope you will be less sugar and more spice,
And only a little bit nice.
Embrace your crunchiness, girls,
Your crustiness, your passions, your selves.
Retain your sparkle, your individuality, your eccentricities. . . .

You need't be ladylike to be a woman,
For being female is complex,
An essence encompassing all that is you . . .
Kind, thoughtful and generous of heart
But honest and fierce and resolute.

—Bobbi Linkletter

Uppity girls. Not obnoxious girls—uppity girls, who see and think clearly and know how to handle themselves and life. Girls who don't fade and disappear into the woodwork. Raising your daughter to be "honest and resolute" challenges you as a parent to be gutsy too. You will help strengthen her inner confidence by allowing her to develop that "spicy" side of her personality, the side that isn't just sugary and nice but makes noise and values her own unique individuality. Give her permission to be passionate about herself and her life; this throws open the doors and windows of opportunity by encouraging her to grow into a fascinating and well-rounded young woman.

She doesn't have to fit the mold to be accepted by others. In fact, the more interesting she is the more other people will be drawn to her. Don't let your daughter get watered-down by life. Help her strive to soar beyond the ordinary, usual, common, and boring. Learning to be cooperative is a skill that your daughter would do well to learn. But, cooperation is about negotiating: working together from a place of individual strength. When she speaks her mind and is clear about her own intentions and opinions she learns how to make good, solid choices and bring strength to any team she is working on. Being saccharine-sweet does not cause others to like her better, it just leaves her in a position of less power because she is not taken very seriously

She has so much to offer: her opinions, passions, energy, and intelligence. Teach her not to be lukewarm. Teach her it's gloriously okay to be fiery, defiant in the face of injustice, intense, ambitious, and unwilling to settle for mediocrity. There are many bright, intelligent, professional women who feel a level of rejection and abandonment because of their drive and intelligence. They wonder whether they should hide their light under a bush. They long to be around people who are captivating and fascinating themselves and are happy to share in the energy and thirst for life that they feel inside themselves. The goal is not to raise daughters that intimidate other people, but to raise daughters that are full of life, energy, vitality, and "crunchiness" that they are not afraid to show!

THE TROUBLE WITH HAMSTERS

I have always loved hamsters. The irresistibly cute, soft, and furry little bundles who peer out at you with beady little eyes and twitching noses. They burrow and snooze, and then wrestle with huge chunks of carrot or work to crack open enormous (to them) sunflower seeds for dinner. They try to squish through your fingers whenever you attempt to hold them. Their antics can be absolutely hilarious. They also croak, about every couple of months to be exact. I had a batch of them. One died right after the other, each one cute, adorable, and predictable—each one doomed within a disappointingly short period of time.

Hamsters are also decidedly small-minded—literally as well as figuratively. With a head the size of a nickel, I suppose we can't expect much. But I am also talking about their worldview. They don't seem very adventurous. On the one hand they seem to be fair-

23

ly curious—or maybe that's just the way hamsters look. They stay burrowed up in their chosen corner, sleeping by day and running around in circles on their exercise wheels by night. Their world stays so small. Is it because of the size of the cage? I don't think so. Even in large "tanks" they don't seem to go to the far edges of their world. They don't seem to be very enterprising little creatures. They just go round and round and round on the same squeaky exercise wheel. A wheel of fortune it is not.

Of hamsters and girls

Chances are your daughter is not furry. But, no matter what her age, she is cute, squirmy, funny, and curious. Are we as parents guilty of keeping these girl creatures in a parent-made cage, physically as well as mentally? Do we teach them to think small? Hoping to keep them safe, do we restrict them to little predictable exercise wheels— wheels that don't go really go anywhere, even though they give the illusion of movement? Frenetic movement with no destination isn't going to land our daughters where they need to go. They will keep returning to ground zero.

Hamsters aren't much for venturing out. It's comforting on some level to have something so cute and vulnerable tucked cozily into a corner. But our daughters aren't as fragile as hamsters and it's not helpful to them to have parents who view them as simply cute and vulnerable. For many girls this necessary bravery does not come naturally. Some girls even create self-imposed cages where they convince themselves the world is not safe to move about in; there- fore they let their fears dictate their lives. It becomes harder and harder for them to take risks and learn how to become strong and capable. Or they simply allow boring routines to take over their schedules.

With parental help they can learn to be brave and take risks. Bravery can be self-taught, but that requires a lot of extra work. An easier route is helping her develop courage slowly and systemati- cally by broadening her thinking to dream dreams that are large enough to stretch her mind and challenge her ingenuity. Help her get off the treadmill of the usual, the boring, the sameness. This doesn't mean dropping out of activities that are simply getting a bit routine, it does mean shedding the no-brainers, the boring waste-of-time activities.

Television—the ultimate hamster wheel

Help your daughter attach value to her time! Ditch television and the mindless hours spent staring into a box of moving pictures and sound: hours absorbing insipid sitcoms that are an embarrassing statement of America's apparent embrace of chronic low-level mentality; vacuous hours filled with messages that girls are supposed to be mouthy, obnoxious, vapid, and bratty; messages about dating, sex, adolescence, and abuse that you hope your daughter will not take on. She will, however, if that is what she is exposed to. Try to pick and choose the television shows worth her time: shows that incorporate real and responsible girls and women; shows that respect women rather than kill, abuse, stalk, or diminish them.

Also, shelve the video games and bypass hours of mesmerizing, beeping video games that are incredibly addicting. Try playing just one video game and quitting. It's like the commercial that challenges you to eat just one potato chip. You can't. You have to keep going. It's the same with your daughter. She can't quit that stupid "exercise wheel"—she just keeps going.

Challenge your daughter to stretch her mind and body. Engage her in activities that will stimulate the borders of her brain and stir her muscles into activity. A right of childhood is to be allowed ample amounts of free, nothing-planned time. But don't let her fill them with brain and muscle cell numbing hours of droning television and wasteland games that are the equivalent of watching paint dry.

Your daughter does not have to settle for small cages, small go-nowhere wheels, and small mentality. She can design a life that fits her. She doesn't have to be a loner. She can hang out with friends that will grow with her instead of stagnate or go downhill. She can create an environment for herself that expresses her identity. She can be assured that it is acceptable to think big. Give her ideas wide open space to grow. Your part will be to help her put building blocks of structure around her goals and dreams, taking them step by manageable step to see if they can become reality.

Is her world too small? Does she always want to do the same thing and seem unwilling to try new things? Try to broaden her horizons with other things to do besides the ordinary routines. Work as a family to turn off the television. Brainstorm for other ideas to use the time. What if you didn't have the TV going on in the background when the family is doing other activities such as eating, talking on the phone, or doing homework? The television and other equally numbing electronic toys constrict a girl's world. They relegate her, like the hamster, to monotonous wheels.

Help your daughter out of her cage. Make sure she is given the message that she has the personal strength and parental support to move out into the real world where she can use her voice, her brain, and her body to accomplish important things!

THE POWER OF "NO!"

In my opinion, "Just Say No!" doesn't cut it. It is more complicated than that. Everyday life includes many levels of emotional and intellectual decision making. However, learning to say "no" is of crucial importance. Teach your daughter that it is okay to say "No, I don't want to." Teach her ways to say "no" that are comfortable for her and acceptable to you.

A great time to begin this teaching process is when she is young. When she is going out for a group activity that you will not be a part of, you can begin with a conversation and practice sessions on how to handle a few situations that might come up. Let her know that you will help her figure out how to handle the situations, but that you will not be there to rescue her. Simple everyday events can be turned into important lessons in self-reliance and an opportunity for her to practice good decision-making skills. Run through upcoming events with your daughter and help her think of possible trouble spots where she might be unsure of what to do or how to handle the situation. Give her a booster shot of confidence so she can stick up for herself even if other kids laugh at her. Most important, have her practice exactly what she can say and do. With a plan in place of what to say and do, it will be easier for her to handle surprises. Be creative in your conversations. Let her see that you do not always know how to handle situations—that you are still learning, too. Share with her some incidents you have struggled with and how they turned out. Let her see that you wrestle to define your opinions and take care of yourself.

It can really be helpful to role-play how to handle uncomfortable situations. Role-playing may seem somewhat corny and you may feel silly. When your daughter gets into a tough situation, however, it will be much easier for her to have the confidence to voice a ready-made sentence that she has in mind. Remember that most kids cannot think fast enough on their feet to come up with a catchy comeback or a power-sentence. It's best not to leave it to chance and hope she comes up with something off the top of her head. It is better to have a workable sentence set in place and ready to go on a moment's notice. Try out different scenarios. Then, when she comes home, proud at how she stood her ground and did not get herself into a frightening situation, you can be sure that she is on her way to taking good care of herself.

*GIRL*COTT VIOLENCE AGAINST GIRLS AND WOMEN

It is still perfectly acceptable in this society to slash, stalk, terrorize, rape, assault, hit, dominate, diminish, name-call, harass, tease, abuse, and last but certainly not least, kill girls and women. Much as we like to think this is not so in our enlightened, kinder and gentler nation, the reality is that America has one of the highest crime rates against women than anywhere in the world!

The "entertainment" industry

Raping and assaulting women and adolescent girls is apparently still considered jolly good sport in the entertainment industry. When was the last time you watched a movie, television, or theater, that did not include some form of violence against women? And don't be fooled. This is not about pornographic flicks at the far end of the continuum. This is about everyday television serials and movies and theater viewing. The stuff everyone watches all the time. Look carefully; it's everywhere. It's so subtle, "mild," and casually woven into the dialogue it doesn't even register anymore. Anything can be done with women's bodies in the media. It is considered entertainment to torment women. Entire movies (again, everyday television and theater) are made around the plot line of a successful, beautiful woman being stalked and terrorized by a crazed male who cannot control his behavior. Or an innocent young woman, mother of two beautiful children is brutally murdered and the hero cop has to solve the gory crime. And, incidentally, why do men put up with being depicted as psychopathic killers who have absolutely no behavioral controls? Is it because they are often depicted as being only one, abnormal male? With women, the audience is left with the message that the next victim could be any woman, at any time, for any reason. And so, girls and women walk in fear.

When all this violence and hatred against women slithers off the movie screen and into everyday reality, our neighborhoods, parking ramps, parks, and street corners, everyone acts so incredibly surprised! While the relationship between movie and TV violence and real life violence is hotly debated, what does seem certain is how numbed many people have become to viewing violence. Children and adults alike regularly view violence on movie and TV screens. Count the number of movies (normal, typical movies) you have seen in the last twelve months that did not include at least some form of violence against women, no matter how "small and insignif- icant." Maybe she was just called the usual derogatory names, or maybe a man just grabbed her arm or got a little rough with her. Or more subtle yet, maybe she always had to go along with what her male partner wanted because she was so dependent on him. Then society recoils in horror when the "real life" evening newscast shat- ters our world once again by reporting a for-real, brutal parking ramp rape and murder of a woman on her way home from work. Horror? Yes. Surprise? no!

Owning responsibility

It's time to get real and take responsibility for the playing out of all this violence against women. It is of course true that most people— men and women—have the internal boundaries, controls, and morals not to act out the violence seen on the screens. But, there is an increasingly large population that chooses not to control their behavior—that choose to go get and do what they want, when they want it. Society and all its ills are blamed. The inequities of society definitely play a major role, but the idea of personal responsibility seems to get left by the wayside. I'm not just talking about adult psy- chopathic personalities. I'm talking about young kids—boys and girls. The morals, ethics, and behavior that respect the rights of oth- ers do not get internalized into many young kids today. These kids are opting for the only form of power they see gets results: violence, usually violence against girls and women. And it's not only the boys—girls are violent against other girls. It's almost like a part of a generation is without souls.

It can be argued that no one person can stop the violence against girls and women. The argument can also be make that it is absolutely every individual's personal responsibility to stop the vio- lence. It goes far, far deeper and wider than each person simply not perpetuating the violent acts personally. The majority of people do not march out and commit violent crimes. The majority of people just don't go to all the work of taking a rock solid, every single instance, every single day stance against violence.

Working today to create a violence-free tomorrow

Is this a naive, pie-in-the-sky dream? Maybe so, but a dream we should all choose to pursue. And remember, it's your little girl, too, who is going to grow up and move out into this war zone against women. Brainstorm and role-model for your daughter what you are doing personally to put a stop to the violence. How?

Shop at only those toy stores that ban toy weapons
Minneapolis is fortunate to have Creative Kidstuff, a toystore that refuses to sell toy weapons. This year, they had a toy weapons buy-back campaign where kids could trade in their toy weapons and receive a $2.00 voucher toward purchasing something at the store. Families noted that it sparked good discussions and debates at home as kids made their decisions. Definitely a cool idea!

Turn off the violent "entertainment"
Get gutsy. Watching cruelty toward women makes each and every viewer less of a person. It takes a little piece of our humanity with every viewing. Don't let your daughter (or son) watch movies, videos, or cartoons that are violent in general and violent toward girls and women in particular. Cartoons are not innocuous. They are often more cruel and violent than regular shows. Turn off the insipid daily television sitcoms that put women down, hurt their feelings or their bodies, or treat them less-than-respectfully. Refuse to let your daughter (or son) rent videos with messages of violence against women. Don't be manipulated into renting it because "most of it isn't like that and all my friends have seen it." Stand firm.

Correct every single derogatory slip

Don't let your girls or boys get away with anything that even remotely resembles violence or prejudice against girls and women. It's hard work and takes constant vigilance, but it promotes a clear, powerful message that violence and prejudice against girls and women will absolutely not be tolerated in your home. Ever.

Hold others responsible for their behavior

Role model for your daughter how to refuse to accept disrespectful behavior against girls and women. Contact other parents, teachers, leaders, coaches, and so on when other children are exhibiting violent or disrespectful behavior toward your daughter or any girl or woman.

Refuse to go along with "the joke"

Stop laughing at the insensitive, stupid, abusive jokes made at the expense of girls and women. Teach your daughter to be brave and to respond differently than her giggling classmates. Laughing right along with the gang continues to feed into the message that girls and women are for sport. Sexual or derogatory teasing toward girls is not good-natured fun. It's cruel and it's really not funny. Ask any girl or woman how she feels about being the focal point of these jokes. Ask your daughter to share with you any incidents where she has felt uncomfortable and creepy because of giggling and jokes. Teach your daughter that she does not have to go along with the joking to be a "good sport." Girls don't like being teased for the "attention." If they giggle at being teased it's because they are embarrassed and humiliated and probably don't know what else to do.

"I'm too valuable to be abused. I deserve respect!"

Teach your daughter this affirmation until she has it cemented into the core of her being. Anyone who attempts to abuse her will run into this brick wall of your daughter's self-esteem.

Call violence against girls and women what it is: Abuse

Don't water it down, downplay its significance, shrug it off, ignore it, tell girls and women to "lighten up," laugh, brush it under the carpet, sweeten it, roll your eyes, or walk away. Everyone is personally responsible for ending the violence.

LIVE, ACTION, CAMERA
Videotaping for Fun and Learning

Your video camera can be an ideal, everyday tool for increasing your daughter's self-confidence. Videotaping done frequently and casually can help your daughter become used to being taped and watching herself in daily action. Use the video camera to assist her to prepare for a presentation, to perfect her baseball pitch, or to practice her music lessons; this can provide her with proof of her growing expertise plus it will serve as a casual, usually humorous corrective device. When you let her be in the limelight frequently and with ease, you help her feel noticed and allow her to get a more accurate picture of herself. Girls are often filled with misperceptions about how they look and act. They sometimes create inaccurate, negative impressions in their minds about how the world sees them. They often then are filled with shame and embarrassment. You can help your daughter develop a casual ease in presenting herself through pictures and videos in a variety of settings and situations. Let her control the camera shots and timing. Let her be in charge of her learning process.

Younger girls relish the chance to be on camera. You can also tickle their fancy with audio cassette tapes. They can sing, tell stories, recite poems, and tell jokes. The tapes will be filled with peels of their hilarious laughter as they spin into their own world of private entertainment. They also enjoy being taped while performing their current talent.

Older girls can exchange audio or video "letters" with friends and relatives. While learning to speak into a microphone they are deepening their vocal confidence and honing their skills of articulating their thoughts and dreams. Seeing for themselves how they look and act will initially cause them to run for cover, but over time they can learn to watch with discerning interest and obtain a more realistic version of how the rest of the world sees them. This is not to make them "more presentable." In fact, just the opposite. The goal is to help her feel natural and comfortably at ease with herself and her body as she is.

Also, exposing her to "real" media experiences is beneficial. Seeing the working insides of television and radio studios as well as newspapers, publishing houses, and print media organizations are a way to pique her interest in finding and using her own voice and talents. The goal is never to embarrass, but always support the actions, talents, and experiments of your daughter. Help her see herself in a positive light that deserves the recognition a camera can bring. Provide her with opportunities to be at ease; it goes a long way in filling her with confidence when the time really does come to perform for all the world to see. She will be prepared, confident, and eager to show off her stuff!

ESTABLISHING POSITIVE
MENTORS AND ROLE MODELS

Imagine your daughter corresponding with a world-famous woman scientist, or receiving a phone call from her favorite author or shaking hands with a woman who is a powerful and influential political figure. When you show your daughter how to find mentors at an early age you give her a skill she can use for the rest of her life. She will know how to meet and communicate with women who have power, intelligence, and energy. Women performing their life's work provide your daughter with a firsthand opportunity to observe and learn. These women may be authors of books or teachers; they may be involved in community or worldwide activities or quoted in newspapers. She can find them virtually anywhere a woman is perfecting her art of living. Help your daughter to contact these women. Show her how to develop a relationship with a role model/mentor who interests or intrigues her. People tend to think that "important" people do not or will not make time to respond. I know from experience that often they do take time!

Why go to all this extra effort? Because it gives your daughter an opportunity to make contact and to build bridges with women who can help her think through who she is in this world. What does she think? What does she want to contribute? You can show her how to contact role models who are working with issues that are vitally important to your daughter's world and future. Show her how to be proactive instead of reactive. Maybe your daughter has an idea of her own; she can send up a trial balloon to a woman already involved and active in the field. She may get valuable feedback about her idea.

Any time you can connect your daughter with a positive, female role model, go for it! It is vital to expose her to women who are doing something, taking action, making a difference, or making a statement. You may not necessarily agree with these women. The core idea is to allow your daughter a chance to meet and hear these women and then use the safety of your family to discuss the topics and issues each woman stands for. You should not squash your daughter's budding opinions, even if they are radically different from your own. As she forms her own connections with positive women, the added bonus is that she is learning how to get noticed in a positive way and to aim high!

ATTENDING PRESENTATIONS BY ROLE MODELS

One great way to introduce your daughter to strong, positive women role models is to bring her to meet, hear, watch, and shake the hand of an accomplished woman in person—the real thing. Where do you find these women? Many colleges, organizations, and large associations invite guest lecturers to town to speak at their events. Authors are always out on book tours—giving presentations and signing books. Best of all, these events are often free. These opportunities allow your daughter to come face to face with esteemed individuals and give her a chance to put her finger on the pulse of powerful issues that will shape her future. By age seven, your daughter can sit easily through a one hour presentation, especially if you brief her on this woman's story and work. Impress on her that she is having an opportunity to hear and see a legend—a woman making a difference.

Check the entertainment section of your Sunday paper. Watch for flyers and notices. Read newsletters and get on mailing lists. The opportunities are endless. If they happen to fall during your work hours, try to juggle your schedule and take her out of school. Most schools welcome any opportunity to broaden the learning experiences of their students. Your daughter could write a brief report and present it the next day (another chance to do her own thinking, writing, and presenting).

As your daughter watches these women speak out on important topics she will learn how to get her mind, hands, and voice around her own ideas. She will learn that ideas, values, and issues are important. This way she will experience one type of forum where she can begin to present her own ideas to the world. As she learns about a variety of issues that are vital to the world at large her own creative energy will be sparked; she will be inspired to get involved in positive change!

A Letter a Week

If your daughter sends out just one letter a week to an interesting woman who intrigues her she will soon find her mailbox filling up with exciting letters and responses. Help her locate the mailing addresses of any woman she is interested in hearing from and then help her set up her letter. Her first letters will inevitably be to movie and rock stars, but then, after that initial rush is out of her system, help her expand her network of interesting people. Tempt her with a wide selection of characters ranging from political figures to owners of magazines, from directors of organizations to scientists and judges and explorers: the adventurers of our time.

You can teach her how to keep her eyes and ears open for possible candidates to receive one of her letters. Show her how to hunt up new names. Show her how to get her letter noticed by using artwork, stickers, and stamps. A catchy envelope goes a long way in getting attention.

You can set a special time each week for letter writing. Show her how to share something of interest about herself in these letters and to ask questions that are important to her. Help her realize that not all her letters will receive a response, but to keep writing and see how many responses she can gather each year. Remember, you are teaching her how to get noticed in a positive way. It is exciting to realize how many successful women are interested in providing a helping hand or some words of wisdom and encouragement to your daughter.

HEARING GLORIA STEINEM

I have admired Gloria Steinem for many years. In June 1994 when she came to Minneapolis, I was determined to see and hear her in person. And I was equally determined to take my daughters, then ages six and nine years old. One powerful way to help raise strong daughters is to provide them with the opportunity to see, hear, and meet influential women. Women who are powerfully speaking out—real women who are effecting change. It is not crucial that your daughter completely understand the spoken word, but rather that she see these women artfully, powerfully, and energetically living their lives and speaking their truths. At the same time it is not really about whether you agree with this woman or not. The important piece is that you allow your daughter an opportunity to hear these women and decide for herself what she thinks. Let your home be a safe place to discuss controversial subjects—a place where your daughter can think out loud, experiment with ideas, and know it is safe to disagree. What better place than home to have an open forum in which she can form her own truth about such issues as date rape, sexual harassment, abortion, and the glass ceiling in the marketplace?

And so I took my daughters to see Gloria Steinem—to hear for themselves and to see a living legend. The room was packed, of course. My oldest bluntly asked, "How come there aren't any men here?" Well, in fact there were—some. I'm glad they came.

I expected someone outspoken, thought-provoking, and intellectually provocative. She was that. She was also tender, warm, funny, and sensitive to the issues of the day—the struggles and concerns of the women before her.

She reminded us that there is no one right way for everyone, and that one way of living may not even be right for every stage of our lives. She noted it is all right for us to live different ways in different times of our lives and to capture new choices along the way. She articulated the disturbing reality that although it has become culturally acceptable to raise girls like boys, it is not at all accepted to raise boys to be like girls. She made us recall that at age eight or nine we were tree climbing creatures who then at age eleven or twelve became "female impersonators" and began saying things like, "How clever of you to know what time it is. . . ." or "It's probably just me but. . . ."

Gloria Steinem has come full circle and proclaimed that reaching age sixty means she can be her tree-climbing, free self again, only now she has her own apartment. And, of course, she challenged us to speak out, reminding us that it is even harder not to; for when we don't, the issues will continue to haunt us.

I wished my daughters and I could have stayed to shake the hand of Gloria Steinem, but it was late and the line was long. Yet as we walked to the car, I reminded my daughters that they had seen a woman who had done more to make their lives better than they could ever know. Never forget. What a voice!

MEETING ROLE MODELS AND MENTORS

It's amazing how many ways your daughter can meet positive role models and mentors. It takes a little time and energy but it's worth it. Where can your daughter meet and get in touch with positive, creative women? Everywhere! Several daily events promote healthy, successful, interesting women.

Attend author book signings

Scour the newspapers and watch for flyers at your favorite book-store. Authors go on tour routinely to read and autograph their new books. Take your daughter to meet all her favorite children's authors and see her favorite books come to life! Encourage her to shake the author's hand and say a few words.

Attend children's plays

Attend plays that allow for the audience to meet, mingle, and inter-act with the players afterward and/or have backstage tours. Many children's play companies have the actors and actresses form a receiving line outside the theater auditorium for that express pur-pose. Your daughter will be thrilled—and probably a bit nervous—to shake hands with these kids or adults who were just up on stage performing their craft. She can touch and communicate with the performers, ask questions, express opinions, and make a connec-tion. Your daughter's imagination may begin to experiment with the idea of trying out the field of drama.

Written-word mentoring

Your daughter can be well-mentored through books, letters, E-Mail, newsletters, and columns. The written word is powerful. Expose your daughter to numerous women writers: editorial writers, essay-ists, authors, experts, and activists. She can meet and communicate with these women through writing. Most girls identify with various authors who become mentors-from-afar that show them a slice of life through their writings. I have received great guidance through reading the body of work written by my mentor-from-afar, Dr. Marsha Sinetar. Over the many years that I have pieced together my career—learning to express who I am through my work—Dr. Sinetar's words have woven their way throughout my decision-making process. I owe her much gratitude for being a strong and clear light along my path. Her works ring true for me. She has graciously communicated with me by phone and by letter, yet I have never met her in person.

Purchase tickets for events that promote women

Even if your daughter is only part of the audience, it is very affirming for her to see and experience women in the limelight. Take her to presentations, lunches, and events where successful women are the focus.

Attend information expos, trade shows, conventions, and fairs that promote women

Some themes include women's issues, women's health, careers, and skill-building. Most larger cities have a number of these a year. Your daughter can meet more healthy, active women in one afternoon at an Info-Expo than she might all year on an individual basis. Usually the local media women and other women in highly visible and influential positions are present. This is a prime opportunity to pick up literature, watch presentations, and interact directly, one-on-one with interesting and inspirational women.

Join committees and organizations led by women

Here your daughter can learn the ropes that lead to change and accomplishment. She could join committees that promote social awareness and change or ones that exist simply for developing the lives of girls.

Take classes from experts or professional women

Alone or together, you and your daughter can reap the benefits of knowledge gained by women experts. Pick something really fun for both of you. You usually will have time for a fair amount of interaction with instructors; often a great question/answer/discussion time follows the class. Here she will be able to meet artists, writers, athletes, chefs—you name it.

Develop positive relationships with women teachers and coaches

Don't overlook this straightforward, readily available source of positive, intelligent, creative women who obviously like kids. What a deal! Most teachers are thrilled to have girls in their classrooms who are willing to go beyond the "meets criteria" into the realm of "exceeds criteria." Teachers can be drawn upon to enrich your daughter's educational experiences. They are usually willing to participate in helping your daughter explore the world through extracurricular activities and enhanced learning techniques. Let your daughter's teachers and coaches help her fill out and round out.

Introduce her to women business owners

Patronize stores and businesses owned and operated by women. Ask to speak to the owner and let your daughter shake her hand. This hand-to-hand contact is more powerful than you might think. Girls remember this attention. Your daughter will have the opportunity to identify firsthand what women are capable of accomplishing. Business ownership is one clear and powerful way to demolish the glass ceiling and avoid the sticky floor of the pink-collar ghetto. These visits show her she can start right at the top—start her own business!

Entertain interesting people in your home

Invite guests into your home for dinner who are engaged in fascinating types of work. These could be co-workers, guest speakers to organizations you are involved in, any teacher, people you have come in contact with doing something interesting yourself, touring experts—anyone who strikes your or your daughter's fancy. Everyone thinks that everyone else is so busy they would never want to accept an invitation to your home. I think you'll be pleasantly surprised at how many people are delighted to be invited over and will attend happily. Let your dinner table be a place to exchange great ideas to feed your daughter's mind and soul as well as feed her body.

Participate in a mentoring program

Explore mentoring programs for girls in the areas in which she is interested. Many corporations, businesses, and educational or artistic foundations have mentoring programs for young girls. Here your daughter would be able to work closely with a woman accomplished in her field. Many fields have women volunteers committed to helping young girls to move up in the ranks. These programs can be achieved through scholarships, competitions, or fees for service. If your school district or large, locally based corporations are not familiar with any such programs in your area, you can find additional resources in the reference department at the library.

Common, ordinary, everyday mentors

For instance? Her mother, her neighbor, her grandmother, her aunt. Engage your daughter as you do common, ordinary, everyday tasks. Show her how to do everything it is that adult woman do. Mentors don't have to be top-of-the-world women. Mentors for your daughter can be found at your own back door. As a woman, show her your work. Show her what your interests are. Invite her along to

43

your favorite activities. Let her help you prepare a complicated pro-ject you are working on. Whatever you do, include your daughter.

DON'T FORGET ALL OF THE GREAT MALE ROLE MODELS

While it is important to provide girls with strong women role mod-els and explore ideas on where to find them and the part they play in a girl's life, girls also can grow tremendously by watching and learning from men. Men who are successful and who care about girls can teach your daughter a myriad of skills as well as expose her to career choices that may be less obvious to her.

Going to work with Dad

Girls can also go to work with their fathers. A man can be the one to introduce her to more typically "male dominated" career options. She will have the opportunity to see career choices less-easily avail-able to women. What a great chance to see what everyone does for a living, men and women. She may go to work with her father, a welder, watch him work, try a few basic skills, and decide to become a welder. Or, she may go with her father or uncle to work and watch him all day and decide, "No, this isn't for me." When she goes to work with men she receives an opportunity to see how men and women interact in the workplace. Let her learn about the com-pany or organization her dad works for. Is the president or owner a man or a woman? Are any men in support staff positions? Are any women in the same type of position as her father? As a father, talk to your daughter about how you got your job. What kind of edu-cation or training was required? Do you know of women doing work like he does?

Male role models

The world is full of men who are successfully working for a better tomorrow for us all. Help your daughter take a look at men who are successful at their work. Talk with her about her opinions concerning what this man is accomplishing. Does she agree with his work? Does she have ideas about how to do it differently or better? Also talk with her about what personality traits this man exhibits. Does he show a humanitarian side? Does he care about people around him? Help her see that men can be caring and attentive. Show her that men can be successful careerwise and still be attuned to the needs of family and loved ones.

Talk to her about men who are making a difference: men who use power and energy to effect positive change; men such as former President Jimmy Carter who after retiring from the Presidency has gone on to found The Carter Center, a center to promote and facilitate peaceful negotiations. He also routinely labors with Habitat For Humanity construction crews.

Bring her to hear top-notch men, just as you would bring her to hear women. She has the right to hear and sort out her thoughts and opinions about men. Introduce her to men who pay close attention to the rights of girls and women and who work toward equality between men and women. Teach her to perk up her ears and listen to men as well as women. Teach her to approach men with an open mind. Men can teach her a great many things about life. Be sure she knows some of these great men in the world!

DEALING WITH NEGATIVE ROLE MODELS

A common concern for many parents is the ready availability of negative role models. These negative role models range from rock stars to kids at school, even to relatives.

Parents have a right to be concerned about the powerful impact of these highly visible people in the lives of their daughters. Your daughter may be quite infatuated with one of these people who carries a less-than-positive message. No parent can make these negative role models go away. You cannot insulate your daughter from negative and destructive messages that are not going to disappear. Once your daughter turns on the television, is mobile enough to move around the neighborhood, or attends school, your power of on-the-spot influence takes a nosedive. Parents soon realize that they only hear and are aware of a small piece of their daughter's daily life; what they do hear about has been filtered by a girl who has probably learned to just keep quiet about a lot of things. Moms and dads end up hearing what their daughter wants them to hear and nothing more.

Who's minding the neighborhood?

In some ways it used to be safer for parents to send their daughters out into the world because the schools, neighborhoods, and society often adhered to a stricter code. The world had more of a sense of shared values. Neighborhoods were closer-knit, people were home more, and a definite watchfulness was present. It goes without saying that when we were young, we were watched and directed by a whole host of people we thought of as busybodies but who probably performed a valuable service. We didn't have the personal freedoms then that kids have now. In fact, sometimes we were downright restricted. But we did have more safety and security. People were always aware of what we were up to. The loss of these external controls is both good and bad. Parenting is probably harder without them. In addition to the loss of these watchful people is the influx of powerful, negative messages, information, temptations, and behaviors of those magnetic, visible few whom our daughters can't help but be exposed to.

Moms and dads no longer have all of this outside help in raising their kids. Your daughter probably has a great deal more personal freedom than you did growing up. She is exposed to and is forced to make choices that you never even thought about let alone

46

encountered. Making educated, healthy choices about negative influences is going to be hard for your daughter no matter how well you have raised her. Peer pressure is enormous and an unbelievable number of families allow their daughters to interact with situations that have a high potential for negative results. The people your daughter idolizes, the friends she chooses to hang out with, and the types of media she views all coalesce to form her personality, values and behaviors. We can't control everything our daughters see, watch, read, or experience (and frankly, I wouldn't want to). Personal freedoms provide important growing material for her to learn to make healthy choices for herself. Struggling through decisions and consequences are good, strengthening life experiences for her. Don't rob her of opportunities to learn.

Focusing your energy

Despite your daughter's rights to personal freedom, chances are you want to limit the amount of negative input your daughter subjects herself to. Where can you as a parent most effectively focus your energies to combat negative role models?

Search your own mindset

Are you overly critical of types of role models because you don't understand them? Remember the Beatles, long hair, Woodstock, beads, and candles? Remember how thrilled parents of young adults were with the influence of the sixties counterculture? Are you being your parents all over again? Maybe you need to calm down just a little. Are these role models really promoting cop-killing, drugs, or rape? If so, jump up and down in defiance of these examples. If they are only promoting the 90's alternative-culture philosophy maybe you could relax a little and go with the flow. Try to ease your mind around a little of today's new material. It may be that we're just getting old!

Friendships

Your daughter's friendships are probably the biggest determining factor in the paths of life she will choose to walk down. If she hangs around with negative peers she will be swayed toward irresponsibility and lackluster goals. If your daughter hangs out with energetic kids who care about their future and how their lives are going, she will too. Girls in particular seem to cluster in groups throughout their school years. Pay close attention to who your daughter's friends are. Meet their parents. Encourage your daughter to have these girls over to eat, sleep, play, and work on projects. Try to say "yes" as often as you can (within reason) to your daughter getting together with these girls. You can't dictate your daughter's friendships. That would be neither fair nor appropriate. You can, however, encourage positive friendships. It's especially helpful to connect with the parents of these girlfriends. Work together as a team to promote positive, healthy and fun times. Plan events together, host sleepovers, or invite a good friend along on short trips. Promoting healthy friendships is over half the battle against any negative input your daughter has to handle.

Listen

Don't be so quick to judge until you hear what is so attractive about this negative role model. Try to have casual conversations with your daughter to learn about why she is so mesmerized by this person. Are all her friends enamored of this star? (See the friendship section above!) In her mind, what is so fascinating about the message this person is sending out? Does she agree with what the message is saying? Where does she see this person going in life? Is that direction appealing to her, too? Is she gravitating toward this negative person because she doesn't want to be left out? (This is a horrifying prospect for just about any young girl.) Pick her brain. Try to interpret her thoughts on this subject. They may not make sense to you, but at least you'll know what they are.

Feeling squeezed?

Listen carefully. Read between the lines of what she tells and shows you. Maybe this negative person is so attractive because she or he offers an exciting, new, and higher level of personal freedom. Remember how desperately you longed for more freedom growing up—more privacy and choices? Perhaps your daughter is feeling squeezed. She has outgrown her skin and wants to dabble in the excited and forbidden "underworld." This one is a tough one to handle. A lot of your response will have to be purely a judgment call. Is she simply stretching her wings, striving to be free and independent? Or is she walking straight off a cliff? And remember, you and your daughter will in all likelihood see things completely opposite from one another.

Support

Support her if it's at all possible. If the role model is repugnant to you but not truly dangerous or sick, try to offer her a little of your support. You don't have to sit for hours with her rapturously listening to alternative rock CDs, but you may purchase one as a gift for her (if it's acceptable to you). It will be a sort of peace offering to let her know that you don't like her choices but as long as they are not destructive to her you can cut her a little slack. If it's a friend, invite this person over for dinner. He or she very well may choose not to come, but you certainly will have offered a white flag of truce to your daughter. If this friend does decide to come to your house, be welcoming! Don't get back at your daughter by giving this friend the third degree or the evil eye.

Lay down the law

If you truly believe in your heart of hearts and are clear in your own mind that this person, event, or media piece is destructive, violent toward her or women, or just plain sick stuff, Be a parent and say "no." Lay down the law. Although teenagers tend to be dramatic, nobody is going to die from some boundaries; her life might take a turn for better because of them. Stand up on your principles and hang tight under pressure. You aren't always going to be your daughter's friend. Your job is to be the parent with all its glories, defeats, and tough judgment calls. Be a dad. Be a mother. Do what you feel you have to do and stick to it. No apologies needed.

FIELD TRIPS TO MEET WORKING WOMEN

What exactly is it that grown-up women do? Ask your daughter. Her answers may discourage you. List ten different occupations and ask her if that career choice reminds her of a man or a woman. Again, her answers may make your heart sink. As adults, it may be easy for us to realize that women can work in traditionally male fields. But, for a variety of societal reasons, our young daughters still perceive women in a fairly narrow array of career choices. They need to see and experience women actively doing the vast assortment of tasks and work that is everyday reality.

The Ms. Foundation's Take Your Daughter To Work program is an excellent place to start with your daughter. Many people reacted to the program with the worried response, "What about the boys?" It's not as if boys haven't been given ample opportunity to explore of world of work. Working to support themselves and their families historically has been the mission of men. More to the point is that this whole idea is not about excluding boys. It's not about boys, period. It's about girls. Why is that so scary for so many people? Girls historically have had very little opportunity to venture out into the marketplace to explore options. Girls need to be made aware of the realities of time, work schedules, job sharing, day care, rates of pay, and types of work. Remember, our daughters don't just automatically know this information. They need to learn about career tracks, unemployment, résumés, and job interviews.

Press on. Ask your friends and colleagues if your daughter could visit their place of work and meet some of the women there. Introduce your daughter to the fact that some women work out of their homes or their cars as well as in offices and organizations.

Show her that women can design flexible scheduling or job-sharing as a way to work out the realities of life's responsibilities. Help her walk through a typical day of a working woman, including before and after work. Include not only the "what-are-we-going-to-have-for-dinner" dilemma, but also consideration of who is going to plan and make dinner, do the laundry, clean up the kitchen, and give the kids their baths. Let her be involved in the planning process of the work/home agenda for her own family. She will need the practice. Perhaps it is time to assess her own level of responsibility. Is she helping out? What are her responsibilities? Having her own personal responsibilities and not having everything done for her will begin to teach her the skills of juggling work and school and home. It is never too early to expect her to make her own bed, pick up her stuff, or help in the kitchen. Expand her horizons of thinking about how the work-home connection plays itself out in day-to-day reality.

Introducing even very young girls to working women helps them establish a foundation on which to build their own career identities. It allows them to grow up with the same message that boys have always had—that grown-ups need to earn a living to support themselves and their families. Teach your daughter early that no one is going to pay her way in life. Let her meet women who are out there in the work world. It is a perfect chance for her to see the wide variety of career choices available to her.

YOUR DAUGHTER THE MENTOR

In your quest to find positive, successful mentors for your daughter, don't overlook your own daughter! As she gains skills, hones her talents, and achieves levels of success, she too can become a mentor for other girls! Think about it. What could be more affirming than a younger girl looking up to your daughter? If she has mastered a subject or a sports event or if she has simply been around the block, she can turn back and take the hand of a younger girl and show her the ropes.

Many schools now have mini-mentoring programs. For example, some schools have programs where older students befriend younger children on the busses. The older students "protect" rather than pick on the younger kids and school bus incidents drop dramatically. Another example is schools that team up a kindergartner with a fifth grader. Together the buddy-teams do fun projects. They also engage in serious learning projects such as the older child listening to the younger child read, or the older child helping the younger with simple math problems and spelling. Some schools even send older elementary, middle, and high school students to inner city preschool programs to build bridges of support and communication between different age groups. Participating in this type of program would bring your daughter great rewards. She would have fun; she would benefit from learning how to make learning fun. It also teaches her the skills of teaching and passing on important information. The kids will form a solid bond over the year and both will start to feel needed and a sense of belonging together. Even meeting together once or twice a month cements in place their working relationship.

Whenever your daughter can volunteer to assist a grown-up with any form of teaching, she is increasing her communication skills and building up her own self-confidence and esteem. As your daughter teaches another child she will deepen of her own level of knowledge. She will have to increase her own skills and understanding to present the material to someone else. She can become the expert.

Your daughter can also become a mentor outside the school classroom. As she masters skills and talents she can pass them on to those coming up in the ranks. This can be a younger sibling, a girl just joining the sports team, the newcomers to an organized group, or any situation where a gap exists between her skills and the abilities of others. Teach your daughter the skilled balance between offering to help those who need it and letting them struggle on their learning path. If she is particularly smart, she may be way ahead of her peers. It's important that she learn the gracious art of supporting others while not making others feel inadequate. Some of that is simply honing her social skills. When she is young, her pride and tendency to crow about herself may be a bit overwhelming, but this is good! She is finding and using her voice. And remember, it's a process. Give it time and gentle guidance. Let her crow!

Mentoring also gives her an opportunity to be in the limelight, to taste what it is like to be the expert. Mentoring often requires a girl or woman to present material in one form or another. This requires her to organize her thoughts in a linear fashion, to be clear on the required steps to get from point A to point B. She will have to back up and figure out how she got her results. This is good practice for future problem solving.

DEVELOPING PHYSICAL STRENGTH AND PERSONAL SAFETY SKILLS

All parents have moments of clutching, nameless fear for their daughters' safety. You look in on her as she is sound asleep and feel a rush of gratitude that she is home safe for one more day and night. And yet you wonder what she may have encountered during the day. Is she ever hassled in the hall at school? Is her confidence eroding from being left out or teased? Does she shrug her shoulders and walk away if you ask her if she has ever been the target of sexual or racial jokes or unwanted advances or teasing?

The world has become a dangerous place. We used to get in trouble for chewing gum. Today, kids bring guns to school—and use them. Danger is everywhere. The buses, malls, freeways, and hallways at school—even the places you like to think are safe don't come with a guarantee.

Unfortunately, safety is an illusion. You can't ultimately guarantee safety from evil people who prey on children or from heartbreaking accidents. In addition, your daughter's own perception of her body will probably worsen during adolescence. Often their physical self-image becomes a mine field of dissatisfaction and distrust. What can you do to protect your daughter in a sometimes overpowering, rough, and insensitive world? Preventive medicine!

Body image

When working with your daughter on developing a positive body image, start by getting a sense of how she feels about her body. Body image and self-esteem go hand in hand. Most little girls feel just fine about their bodies. They love to go streaking through the house after their baths. Feeling exhilarated by their strength they can run like the wind. They think they're hot stuff. And they are. Then as they get older, slowly but surely, they start to pick their bodies apart.

Ask your daughter questions. Is she afraid of her body getting hurt? Is she concerned her body won't work right? Is she worried that she is getting fat? Do her peers tease her about how she looks? It is worth asking her because she may be thinking she needs to go on a crash diet while you think she's skinny as a beanpole. Your perception of her body and her perception of her body may be worlds apart. Begin by going on a fact-finding mission. It may take a few days or a few weeks of casual conversations and observations but the information you gather will be worth the effort.

Feeling comfortable with her body and knowing her body will be there for her when she needs it is a goal worth achieving. As a parent you can begin early to help her see her body in a positive light. All too early, many girls begin to worry about weight, hair, and clothes. They begin to concern themselves with how they appear to others, rather than focusing on an internal level of comfort. Teaching girls to be creative about their bodies is a monumental task. If begun too late, it's ten times harder. That she wants to look great is natural; it makes sense that she wants to pay attention to her body. An obsessive focus on outward appearances, however, can be a sign of trouble brewing. The point is to view developing a good body image as a philosophy of life. A lifestyle. It is not a one-size-fits-all venture. Each girl must come to grips with the body she has.

Personal safety

As parents, moms and dads need to be strong, vocal advocates for their daughter's safety and well-being. They must be willing to contact the school principal and the police department when even small, disquieting incidents take place. The even harder task is monitoring your own daughter's behavior. No parent wants to think his or her daughter would shoplift, skip school, or try drugs. "Not my daughter—she wasn't raised that way." Girls' actions are due not only to how they were raised, but also to the forceful, peer-pressured world in which they move every day. Don't wait for something hideous to happen and then kick yourself. Get and stay involved in your daughter's life. Be alert to the circle of friends she moves in. Get to know the other parents. And always keep repeating your family rules for personal safety.

You can learn everything possible about safety precautions, but more important you must systematically teach and enforce priority safety rules. Show your daughter how to be her own best advocate for her personal safety. Help her practice what to say and what to do in a variety of situations. Remember, you aren't doing her any favors if you don't enforce the safety rules you have set up for your family. She must learn the seriousness of personal safety. And you must take incidents of harassment and all safety threats seriously while you teach her how to demand respect for her body and her space.

Adolescents in particular have a rather glorious sense of immortality. Your daughter will be quite absurdly convinced that nothing bad will ever happen to her. Other girls might get pregnant, but somehow, magically, she won't. Other kids might get hurt in car accidents, but for some strange reason, it won't happen to her. You probably won't be able to convince her of any of this, but you can at least teach and prepare her to handle the meaner side of life. Pretending this side doesn't exist simply increases her chances of getting hurt. Knowing what to do in a bad situation will increase her chance for getting out of it safely.

Safety at home is another aspect to consider. Your daughter needs privacy zones. Adapt to her changes, respect her wishes as she matures, and teach her siblings to do the same; it will go a long way to strengthen the communication between her and the rest of the family.

When your daughter is young you can protect her from many dangers—often by just picking her up and carting her off. But as she grows and ventures out farther and farther into the world, your control slips away at an alarming and unsettling speed. Daughters must be prepared to handle danger, confusion, trickery, and cruelty. As a way to address the unpleasantries society provides, you can help her become involved in organizations and groups that address these issues and work to bring about local and global peace and harmony.

As we hope and pray for our daughters to stay safe, we can also with fierce determination teach girls to be strong and to protect themselves as best they can in a less-than-perfect world.

LEARNING EVERYDAY HOME MAINTENANCE SKILLS

Helping your daughter be comfortable with her body includes showing her how to perform basic household maintenance tasks. It is important to show her how something works and let her actually try it, rather than just telling her what to do. Although maintenance skills require that she use her head, they also allow her to test her physical capabilities and learn how good it can feel to perform everyday maintenance tasks.

Next time you stop to get gas for your car, let your daughter pump it. Show her how to read the register and work the pump. You can also watch "how-to" television programs together. Shows such as "Martha Stewart Living," "This Old House," and "Victory Garden" are informative, interesting, and filled with great ideas about activities you and your daughter can do together. Also, take her to the annual Home and Garden Show, Boat Show, and Auto Show. Let her touch, feel and experience a variety of mechanical objects.

Show your daughter how operate the lawn mower, the snow blower, and the circuit breaker in your fuse box. Let her actually do it so she can experience it firsthand. Show her how to check and add oil to the car. Let her pour it in. It does not matter if she is only ten years old and can't drive a car. Teach her about the car, how to pump air into the tires, change a tire, or change a windshield wiper. Help her appreciate the work that goes into maintaining a well-running car. Someday, she is going to own one; she shouldn't have to depend on her dad or boyfriend to take care of her car's basic needs. Show her how to change doorknobs and locks, measure and hang pictures and window coverings, and varnish a window sill. The goal is not only for her to be able to complete a task when she needs to in ten years (although that in and of itself is a perfectly good reason), it is also to increase her sense of confidence in her body's ability to perform different types of tasks.

If you are a homeowner, each season provides opportunities to teach your daughter about different pieces of household equipment. Show her how to inspect the fireplace, how to check the condition of the roof and how to clean out the gutters! Bring her along when you buy weed and feed for your lawn. Let her watch while you install a light fixture; explain how to use the power drill. Have her change the film in the camera and program the VCR. Girls grow up into women who need to understand and handle household maintenance. Every time you do any household task show your daughter how to do it. It doesn't matter whether you live in an apartment, in a mansion, or with other family members. Show her what she needs to know to run an efficient, well-maintained household where she does not have to depend on someone else to solve her problems.

PRIVACY AT HOME

As girls mature, they require more privacy. Sometimes, they want so much privacy it drives the rest of the family nuts. They hog the bathroom, carry on about having a "bad hair day," write thousand page diaries, and have a fit if you hear their phone conversation.

The concept of personal boundaries becomes particularly important as girls approach puberty, the turning point of adolescence. One way to think of boundaries is as the fence and gate we keep around ourselves that separates us from others in a positive, healthy way. It is important to teach your daughter to be in charge of her personal space, to decide who she wants to be a part of her life, and to discern who, when, and how she will let others touch her. Learning good boundaries is learning to develop control over her private space. It is learning to prevent others from trampling on her or dumping "trash" into her life space. It requires that your daughter know what her own needs and wants are.

The increased need for privacy begins around fourth grade and continues to intensify as she heads toward middle or junior high school. This need for privacy is acute. Just as each family has its own set of rules, each family will have to decide how best to handle these new requirements. For example, a girl has a right to be left alone in the bathroom. Siblings (particularly brothers, but other family members as well) do not have the right to barge into the bathroom when she is in there. Rules may need to be established about the amount of time she can take, but her privacy must be respected. (Then again, you may want to consider installing one of those portable toilets out behind the garage for the rest of the family to use. . . .) The same goes for bedrooms. It is not okay for other family members to open closed doors without knocking, go through her private drawers, or see her or touch her when she is not fully clothed without her permission. She has an absolute right to privacy of her body and the space around her.

Your daughter's personal space includes her letters, mail, and diaries. Parents are tempted to sneak a peek at her private archives to gather information that is hard to come by the older she gets. Tampering with her personal material, however, will only bring destruction to your relationship with her. She has a right to privacy that should not be violated just because she is smaller than you. Think how you would feel if she got into your personal correspondence and read your personal and private words. Only if you honestly believe she is involved in something illegal or clearly self-destructive do you have the right to override her right to privacy. If you do violate her personal writings, be prepared to be the recipient of her wrath as well as her decreased trust in you!

Some girls also hide objects. For some odd, inexplicable reason, my oldest daughter when in preschool used to collect bits of debris off the floors at her daycare center. She would gather up tiny pieces of string, bits of paper, and her favorite—dust bunnies—and deposit them in her cubby space. Over time she managed to compile a rather complete collection, the envy of any two-year-old. Obviously some kids are born packrats. This habit is amusing as well as frustrating, but it is reasonably harmless. Children may hang onto every birthday party favor, book mark, and plastic toy won at the carnival. (Incidentally, these girls get quite a kick out of semiannual, blowout cleaning sessions. They burst with pride at their ability to fill two to three garbage bags full of paper to recycle and junk to throw out. It's useless, however, to try to get them to part with their collections on a regular or routine basis. They won't!) More seriously, some kids hide things for a variety of less humorous reasons. They are afraid of being found out that they have "contraband" in their possession. Again, her room is her room. If you truly believe there is a valid reason to search, then you need to do what is necessary to get to the bottom of the issue at hand. Acting as though you don't know she has drugs, cigarettes, or shoplifted merchandise is doing her a grave disservice. If you're just curious, try to stay clear and don't snoop. It's not fair to her.

Young girls who are not yet beginning to mature have a basic right to privacy as well. Closed doors need to be respected.

Decisions need to be made about when your daughter should no longer be sleeping with or showering with her father or brothers. Girls need to begin early to define the boundaries of space and privacy that are their right. Families are the best place to teach girls respect and good boundaries.

One last thought (and this may seem like a stretch, but I'm not so sure that it is): It's the tiny, constant, everyday messages given to your daughter as she is growing up—messages that she has a right to her privacy, personal space, and complete authority over her body—that she can draw on later when she is dating and perhaps feeling pressured by boys. If she has learned early on about privacy and the right to personal space from a family that firmly respected her space and body she will be able to clearly say "No, this is my space, my body, my room, and I'm in charge of it!" She will have had the opportunity to practice with her family for many years before she is in a situation where she is on her own and needs to stand her ground. Once these boundaries are firmly ingrained in her thinking and beliefs, she will have them readily at her command.

SPORTY FAMILIES

Families that play together stay together. Girls who exercise feel better about their bodies—more confident and sure of themselves. They learn they can rely on their bodies to be there for them. They feel strong and know how their bodies work. The more they use and feel comfortable with their bodies, the more physically at ease they will be. Their bodies won't be a mystery to them. Many girls still shy away from their bodies and feel ill at ease when they have to stretch and push their bodies to do more and different activities. They feel embarrassed in gym and ashamed of their bodies.

If your family works together to get physically fit, your daughter will have a natural place to begin feeling more comfortable with using her body. As a byproduct, she will also become more physically fit. Families can easily get involved together in exercise and sports activities. There is more to sports than plopping down in front of the TV to watch seasonal sports. It is fun for the family to gather to watch the big football games, summer and winter Olympics, and special sporting events, but getting up off the couch and making exercise a family affair teaches her good skills and habits.

You may be thinking, "Oh, yuck!" Right? Well, there's hope even for nonexercise people. There are some great ways to get and stay in shape as well as a wide variety of activities that are easy and just plain fun and don't even seem remotely like exercise. Curious?

"Real" exercise

Real exercise is the stuff you do in exercise clothes that tends to make you work up a sweat. You'll know it when you've done it. You can also do real exercise in any comfortable outfit you have: jeans, T-shirts, or sweatsuits. It's much more fun if you all go together. What to do?

Put on comfortable clothes and pop a Kathy Smith video in the VCR, or any funky exercise video

Do it together. Roar with laughter as you all attempt to pull off what the instructor manages to do with such ease. Or, if you don't have a VCR (or even if you do), set a time two or three times a week to go on a very brisk walk—not an after dinner stroll, major walking! Take the dog, the kids, the neighbor's kids. Or get on your bikes once a week and ride around the neighborhood park or lake. Feel it in your legs. Give your lungs and heart a workout. Push yourself just a little more each time.

Find an exercise room

If you're not into spending $25,000 to add an exercise room onto your house, go out and find one. Join an exercise club. They are not all extremely expensive. Get a family membership at the YMCA or YWCA or go to your local school district's community center. They often have a gym, a swimming pool, and other assorted exercise rooms. For a small fee you can play to your heart's content. A night in the swimming pool can cost as little as $8.00 for a family of four. You spend a lot more than that on greasy fast food!

Join a sports team

A myriad of sports teams are available for your daughter or your family to join. Encourage her to join a team. She could pick soccer, basketball, softball, bowling, swimming, tennis, gymnastics, dance, skiing, or ice-skating to name just a few. She is bound to enjoy some of these activities. The benefits of joining a team extend far beyond just the physical exercise. She will learn about team spirit, competition, sharing, sportswomanship, confidence, and self-esteem. She will have to struggle a little, work hard, get hot, deal with defeat, and taste triumph. The cost for joining house teams or local playing teams is rather inexpensive, well under $100. Traveling teams tend to cost quite a lot more. You and your daughter can decide what fits for your family.

Your daughter will have great memories from joining and sticking to a sports team. You as a parent could consider volunteering to coach one of these teams. It would be a great opportunity to spend time regularly with your daughter and role-model good team building and social skills. The position she plays will be important and it will matter to the rest of her team. As she works hard not just for herself but for the team she will experience a sense of belonging. What a natural for many dads!

Super easy exercise

Exercise the easy, casual way.

Have company over who bring their kids. After dinner grab all the kids and any willing grown-ups, the family dog, the neighbors, any and all willing participants and rustle up a game of volleyball in the back yard or basketball in the driveway or bombardment in the front yard or softball wherever there's room. No yard? Go down to the park or an empty lot in your neighborhood.

Does it snow where you live?

Don't just take the kids sledding and ice-skating and then go pick them up. Put your own skates on. You can rent skates at any rink. Your daughter will howl with pleasure watching you teeter around on skates. Or put some warm jeans on and get on that sled yourself! Your daughter will be in heaven and will fight to be the one to go down the hill with you. This is serious exercise by the way. Have you walked back up any of those icy-snowy hills lately? The first few times are no problem—piece of cake, lots of fun. But then that hill starts to get bigger and slipperier every time you trudge back up it. Your daughter isn't the only one getting her exercise.

No snow?

Go swimming. Put your suit on and jump in. Don't just sit poolside with your shades on sipping a soda. Get in the water with your daughter. Play with her. Go down the water slide. Be a kid.

Take a weekend afternoon and go hiking in a national park

Bring a picnic lunch and wear your comfortable jeans and shoes. In most parts of the country, autumn is exquisite. But then so is spring. Turn it into a seasonal tradition. Get your pumpkins (even if she's sixteen, she'll be drawn to carve it), buy apples, and collect natural decorations to make her room homey and seasonal.

Go bowling

There are lot of circus-type bowling lanes cropping up. You get the whole nine yards: bowling, snacks, real food, games, and prizes. These places work well for birthday parties, too.

Go grocery shopping!

Yes, as part of your physical fitness agenda, go grocery shopping as a family. Not all the time, but every once in a while. Plan your list ahead of time to include healthy foods that you want to add to your menus. Think about what foods will accomplish your goal of a healthy, low-fat, low-cholesterol diet. Planning is half the battle to creating healthy eating habits. Teach your daughter how to plan her eating in conjunction with a healthy physical exercise program.

Good exercise isn't hard to accomplish. It doesn't even take that much preplanning. Just be mindful of opportunities and grab them whenever you can. The formal planned exercise times and sports teams are great for developing strength, skill, and good physical habits. But the informal, spur-of-the-moment games and activities are just as important and can be great fun.

THROW AWAY THE SCALE

Sometimes I think there should be a law against home weight scales! Society drives home the message to girls and women that toothpick thin is the height of perfection. A girl cannot pick up a magazine without seeing pictures, articles, and recipes that tell her how to lose weight. Beautiful, healthy girls find themselves feeling fat and ugly based on unrealistic expectations pushed on them by the media.

Eating disorders are a major problem for today's young girls. Issues of dieting and fat already have a foothold by the time girls reach elementary school. Ten-year-old girls examine their bodies in the mirror and frown with displeasure. Adolescent girls look to magazines for fat-free recipes and are making their dietary decisions based on what some supermodel eats in a typical day, which often is next to nothing and is usually a starvation-level diet.

Eating disorders are really about control. Opinions differ on what provokes them; why some girls have them and others don't; why girls who seemingly have it all: confidence, attractiveness, smarts, "good" families have truly poor body images. These girls for one reason or another begin to become overly conscious of their food consumption. Often it starts innocently enough, with a girl deciding to eat more healthy and natural foods. But slowly a line gets crossed and she begins to obsess about food. She begins to "feel better" if she doesn't eat much. She begins to cut her portions in half. She begins to focus on one food in particular and doesn't like to mix and match foods at one time. After a while she begins to lose weight and she thinks "This is great! I'm not so fat!" Then over time her friends start to notice she doesn't eat the pizza, chips, and hamburgers that everyone else is eating. Again, she feels somewhat proud, if frustrated, that they don't just leave her alone about it. This girl is anorexic. She has probably already lost ten to twenty pounds and she has skipped one to three menstrual periods. She may be starting to get worried about herself but she can't get her thinking back on track. She can't stop thinking about food. Why? Because she is starving herself. Her body is crying out for nourishment and substance. She thinks she can only eat one half an apple on a given day, so she has to plan when she can have another later in the week. Thus the cycle is cemented in place; a tiny amount of food and the rest of the day spent obsessing on when she can have a tiny bit more. Proud of her ability to resist food and happy with her dropping weight, she is oblivious to the fact that even her face and arms are looking bony.

The flip side of the eating disorder coin is bulimia. This girl stuffs herself, feels guilty and physically horrible and gets rid of the food, usually through vomiting, laxatives, spitting it out, or flip-flopping into starving herself for a few days. The pain and guilt is overwhelming but she too obsesses about food and how it feels once it is inside her body.

Often these girls need a professional outside of the family to help them over the hump and back on the track of healthy thinking as well as eating. Family members may be too close and involved to provide her the foundation and nudge for change that she needs. Shaming, fear tactics, and unrealistic demands to eat never work. These girls need a sense of real control to make their own healthy decisions.

If your daughter seems to be moving in the direction of obsessive eating or dieting help her regain control over her decisions. Explain to her that when she binges on food or starves herself, she is in fact not in control, the disorder is. Only when she makes healthy, clear choices about what to eat, is she actually in control. It is also helpful for her to say out loud or quietly to herself as she creates her meals, "I choose to eat _____ (whatever)", giving herself the message that she gets to be in charge of her eating, not the disorder or her parents, her doctor, or anyone else.

Encourage her to keep a meal diary, planning ahead if possible or at least writing down what and how much she ate. Following her food list have her write her feelings about eating and how she feels after eating. This is where a professional counselor can be very helpful, because this counselor can help your daughter process her feelings and reactions in a way a parent alone probably cannot.

Help your daughter learn to listen and read her internal body signals; this will lead to a much healthier approach to fueling her body than watching the numbers on a scale go up or down. When she eats when she is hungry and/or when she chooses she will free herself to enjoy the pleasure of food and keep it in its proper perspective. Food can be an very enjoyable aspect of life; no young girl should have to spend extra mental energy thinking and obsessing about it. If we model good eating habits and natural weight control for our daughters, who really needs a scale? Let's start a new trend: National Trash Your Home Scale Day! An annual event to free girls and women from the tyranny of imposed skinniness!

BODIES GROWING UP

SEX. I got your attention didn't I? Well, every year that fascinating little subject is going to get more and more of your daughter's attention, too. Each family needs to decide for themselves how they want to handle the discussion of sex and sexuality, but this discussion really needs to happen. The more you can matter-of-factly address it, the easier it is in the long run. The subject is going to come up whether your daughter is three or sixteen. I have informed my two daughters that they may date and/or get married when they are forty years old, and not before. I'm glad I have cleared that up with them and that they clearly understand. Because they roll their eyes and give me a dismissive "MOOOOM!" I'm not sure they take me seriously, but I feel better knowing they will be safe and sound for another thirty years!

Seriously, talking about sex, sexuality, and your daughter's body is really not hard. It just takes comfort on your part, a willingness to listen to her, and an open mind.

Her changing body

When your daughter changes or discovers something interesting about her body she will naturally begin to wonder about sex and sexuality. I believe that information and education help girls to make informed and educated choices and do not put ideas into her head that would not otherwise be there. Her body should not be a mystery to her. She owns it, needs to be in charge of it, and therefore needs a good owner's manual available to her. When you are matter-of-fact and casual about discussing her body you help her adopt an attitude of wholesome self-respect.

When she is young and streaking through the house laughing and making herself impossible to catch, it's hard to imagine that in just a few short years she may be frowning and scowling at her image in the mirror. It's perfectly all right for her to admire and check herself out in the mirror. The more she can admire her body the better. Her admiration will diminish any tendency toward viewing herself critically. As she grows older and begins to obsess about her hair and clothes, she continues to look in the mirror but is more hesitant to pronounce herself as acceptable. Begin early to admire her. In addition to assuring her that she is cute, beautiful, looks great, and all the usual compliments, admire the strength of her body as well. Even when the comments to her about her body are positive, make sure your entire focus isn't always on her physical appearance. It is too easy in this society for girls and women to put all of their emphasis on beauty and attractiveness. Her worth is not tied to her beautiful looks. Include in your compliments statements that tell her she is looking strong and graceful. Point out her long fingers, smooth muscles, strong arms, and clean skin. Help her to be aware of her body from a positive perspective, focusing on her strength as well as her attractiveness. Being in a girl's body is more than just being attractive. It is about being strong, healthy, vigorous, and mighty.

As her body changes, help her thoroughly understand what's happening and why. Spare no details. She has a right to know. Keep it simple and easygoing. Each "first experience" she has as a girl will be a bit nerve-racking for her. Keep your sense of humor; try not to get irritated with her. Buying first bralettes, feminine hygiene products, deodorant, and the like can be done after you've had a comfortable discussion well in advance of her actually needing these supplies. Leave it up to her to begin using these things as she feels ready. Keep it easy and casual. Sometimes she feels the need to have and use these items just because her friends are using them. She may not need them but feels more like she is part of the group if she does. No harm in wearing a little something extra if it makes her feel like she belongs to the big world of womanhood.

Important topics of discussion

It's so much easier to handle the really big subjects if you casually have been discussing the smaller stuff along the way. It's important that you work through your own discomfort, embarrassment, and feelings about sex and sexuality so that you can talk to your daughter with ease, dignity, and humor. You will need to discuss big topics over time; it's not helpful if you slide under the table every time they're brought up. Be available to get into great discussions with your daughter about her thoughts on abortion, rape, dating, sex, babies, boys, AIDS, STD, kissing, and other hot topics. Listen while she sorts out her opinions; try not to judge. Judging and anger will only shut down the conversation. Give her accurate and clear information. Try to speak freely and openly about all sexual topics. If your six-year-old is in on the conversation between you and your ten year-old, great. She can learn to think and speak about sexual topics with comfort instead of skulking around and getting atrociously bad information from her friends. Plainly state the reality of being sexual. State information pointblank and ask direct questions so she clearly understands the realities. This is not about making pronouncements but about offering clear information and food for thought. Be clear about such things as the fact that she can get pregnant the first time she has sex, and anytime thereafter. A mindboggling number of girls are surprised when they find out they are pregnant. They understand how it happens, they just can't believe it happened to them.

When you keep the topic of sexuality out in the open for easy discussion you demystify it for your daughter. It's a lot easier for her to make healthy decisions at crucial moments when she has been over this subject a million times at home.

What's it really all about?

Girls take their changing bodies as the most serious issue of their growing up. Parents take their daughter's budding sexuality as the most serious issue. As with most issues, growing girls may think they understand it all and know everything there is to know about everything. In fact, girls will not truly understand what sex and sexuality are really all about for a long, long time. It's something that develops with wisdom and time. This lack of true understanding can cause a myriad of dilemmas for girls who are sexually active. They may enter into sexuality for a variety of reasons, none of which are really healthy for them. The difficulty is if your daughter is already sexual, she probably is not going to stop, even though at her early age in all likelihood she doesn't really even enjoy it all that much. Girls often confuse attention with sex. Keeping boyfriends, doing what friends do, following the media model all push her into becoming sexually active well before she is truly ready. Slowing your daughter down is a lot harder than postponing her sexual debut. Fourteen-year-old girls aren't really looking for sexual expression, they are looking for love, attention, cuddling and someone to connect with. Parents can certainly prevent daughters fifteen and under from becoming sexually active. Later as girls begin to date and develop relationships parents still cannot look the other way. Girls who have chosen to become sexually active despite parental intervention need education and information about how to prevent pregnancy. Adolescent sex is not representative of what sex really is. True sexuality comes much later. Teens don't comprehend this. It's a losing battle to try to impress upon them that they don't know what they don't know. Prevention of sexual activity is a better and more effective route to take.

ABOUT TOWN

Everyone gets lost in the car or on foot from time to time. It can be frustrating or funny depending on the situation. When you help your daughter to learn her way around this world of ours you teach her skills she can use to find her way home from a football game or to get around France as a foreign exchange student. Once she understands the basic skills, she can figure out how to get "home" for the rest of her life.

When your family is planning a trip, be it day trip to a state park or a two week vacation abroad, engage your daughter in the planning stages—not only to plan the highlights, but also to figure out the routes. She can help figure out airline flights, train schedules, highways, and scenic routes. If you are using a travel agent, bring your daughter along to learn the process.

As you travel throughout your city, familiarize her with landmarks. Show her how to understand how to get from point A to point B. It's fun for an elementary school kid to be the one to read the street signs and tell you when to turn. When she is older and driving herself, have her drive whenever the family goes anywhere (as long as she is not too tired or frustrated). You will have a chance to watch and improve her driving skills as well as help her to rely on her own navigating skills.

It is important that she understand how to reach her destination. Learning a particular route by memory is fine to help her get to her friend's house. However, when she is in the South of France some-day, or in New York City, and she is hungry and tired, memory won't do her much good. Learning to travel is an incredible opportunity to teach her to become a world citizen, a girl and later a woman who knows her way around. Traveling builds confidence, ease, flexibility and citizenship. Learning to find the places she needs increases her confidence and knowledge that she can take care of herself.

But you don't have to travel to Europe this summer to teach her these beginning skills. It's really quite easy to weave these skills casually into daily life. Every time you drive past a lake or a river, ask her which one it is. At first she will blurt out any name she has heard in the past. Show her how to look for road signs that often provide clues. For example, the boulevard around a lake often bears the name of that lake. A bridge often holds the name of the street it connects.

Does your daughter know how to read a map? If not, look at maps together. If she is five, she can learn how to spot the lake she passes on her way to school. If she is fifteen, she can plan your route to visit relatives or a college upstate. Don't let your daughter rely on others to get her places. Teach her to figure it out for herself. Teach her basic—but imperative—safety skills about traveling. If she is driving alone late at night, have her wrap her hair in a top bun and put on a baseball cap. (I'm serious, by the way). Tell her to lock her doors immediately when she gets into the car. If you can afford it, buy a cellular phone or CB radio for such occasions. Remember to have to her pay for any telephone air time she uses for personal reasons (see chapter 8). If she is younger and just start-ing to ride her bike away from home, follow her now and then at a discreet distance to make sure she is following all safety rules. This does not mean you should spy on her. Rather, instill in her the seriousness of protecting herself and paying attention to detail when traveling.

Another issue of travel is the reality of getting hungry and tired. Whether you are on a weekend trip or just out shopping for the day, let her figure out where to eat or where to stay and how to get there. Teach her to call ahead for directions if necessary. Help her learn how to forage for food before everyone is starving to death. Then, once you are there, let her figure out the cost of the meal (always keep a calculator in the car). Let her know your budget and let her figure out if you're on target. A special event, such as a state or county fair is a great time to let her figure out how to get around. Let her look at the map handed out at the gate; let her help plan the day, including how to get to the highlights that each person wants to see. This is extra work if she is only seven, but it can be kept lighthearted and fun. It's great if you manage to "get lost" when you're on your trip. Getting lost just begs for a chance to help her learn to retrace her steps, problem-solve, and ask for help when she needs it.

Also, when she is going somewhere for a few days, let her do her own packing. Seven-year-olds can pack a pretty mean suitcase full of "stuff" but it's a good opportunity to help her think through what she needs as well as what she wants. If your ten-year-old is going to camp for a week, let her take responsibility for reading the instruction list for what to bring. If she forgets her toothbrush let her figure out how to get her hands on another one (you may not want to know the gross details on this one). Help her plan ahead and plan to handle the unexpected at a young age; this helps her be ready years later to handle "lost luggage" in Europe with aplomb. She will know the ropes for self-preservation and how to get her needs met at a low-impact frustration level.

Road signs, landmarks, travel guides, and maps are the tools for getting around in this world. Last but not at all least is to teach your daughter to listen to her instincts. Teach her to listen to her body's comfort level, the hair on the back of her neck, that creepy feeling that she went a few blocks too far for comfort. Teach her to see the signs of danger and how to react and bring herself back to safety. Teach her how to stay out of the shadows of life and use all of her senses for personal safety and high adventure!

HANDLING AND AVOIDING HARASSMENT, TEASING, AND UNWANTED TOUCHING

A friend of mine recently told me about something that happened to her eleven-year-old daughter on the school bus. "Sarah" had been sitting in the back of the bus when a group of boys grabbed her school bag, dumped it out and generally harassed and frightened her. She said nothing and waited until she got home and walked into the house before bursting into tears. Her mother called the department of transportation only to be told by the man who answered the phone that "Well, the back of the bus is kind of the boys' turf, maybe your daughter should just ride in the front." In response, my friend had the clarity of mind to state firmly, "Excuse me, but my daughter should be able to ride anywhere on the school bus and be safe!"

So, what is typical school boy/girl teasing and what is not? How do we know where to draw the line and where to just let kids work it out themselves? We can all recall painful experiences from our own childhoods related to walking home from school, hanging out in the hallways, or sitting in the lunchroom. Every girl and woman recalls moments of being tormented, usually having something to do with her girlness. In Sarah's case, because she was surrounded and overwhelmed she was unable at that moment to take her power back. It is not easy for girls to get through the school year without something bad happening to them. As parents, we usually don't even hear about it until long after the fact, if at all. We need to anticipate potential situations and work with our daughters on how to handle them, realizing we may never even know whether they occur.

Teaching young girls the difference between "good touch/bad touch" is good preventive medicine. As they grow older, the lines blur and situations become stickier and less easy to define. Your daughter may find herself feeling creepy or uncomfortable without really knowing why. Often girls are made to feel that they are being ridiculous if they don't go along with teasing, jokes, and touching. Other times girls willingly accept bad touch because they are desperate for affection and attention. Girls can feel pressured to laugh it off. When they do say something it's usually prefaced with, "It's probably just me but . . ." or "I'm probably just crazy but. . . ." Too often girls take the blame for not liking what society dishes out and what society has decided is an okay way to treat girls.

When we look around and see how shabbily kids and adolescents can treat each other, we have to wonder where it comes from. Parents shake their heads and say the kids never learned that language or behavior at home, and that may be true. But we have to wonder who is minding the store when society tolerates so much violence against girls and women. And we have to start in our own corner of the world, chipping away at the cruelty and lack of regard for women and others. Without depicting girls and women as helpless victims, have honest conversations with your daughter about how women are treated in movies. Why are women slapped by their male partners? Raped, or near raped? Called derogatory names? How many videos has she watched in the last year where men treat women as objects but the women still appear to like the guy? It's everywhere! I recently purchased a copy of the *Oliver!* video thinking my daughters would enjoy the musical. My memory about it was fuzzy and so I viewed it alone ahead of time. Midmovie, the male character badly beat the female character, brutally throwing her around the room and to the floor. He then stomped out and she went out on the balcony and sang "As long as he needs me. . . ." It was sickening. The movie went in the garbage. So many abusive movies, so few garbage cans. . . .

Give your daughter opportunities to discuss violence against women. It goes a long way in helping to prevent it. Your discussions give her a chance to air her thoughts and feelings, sort out what she believes about herself and define a code of ethics that she herself practices and expects from others.

How can you help your daughter figure out strong responses to negative situations?

1. Ask her periodically about incidents she has experienced herself or has seen when she was at school or the mall. Check out how she felt and ask her what she wished she could have said. Help her come up with clear, specific responses to that incident. This gives her a basis from which to work in the future. It teaches her how to formulate ideas and sentences.

2. Point out to her negative situations when you see them. Whether you are shopping or at a ball game, when you see something offensive, talk briefly with her—right there, in the thick of things. Brainstorm together what some responses might be if the offensive action were happening to her.

3. Pick up informative pamphlets when you come across them. They are often distributed at doctors' offices, health fair booths, shopping malls, and schools. Read through them together. Remember this information is new to your daughter. Go over it with her and make sure she understands the ideas.

4. Point out the positives. Show her situations and people that are exhibiting healthy, respectful behavior toward women and girls. Tell her about encounters you have had that day that you think role-model right-on behavior toward girls and women.

These are just a few ideas to get you going with your daughter. Use any incident or event to take a moment to teach her that girls and women deserve to be treated respectfully.

PARTICIPATING IN THE WORLD

Did you know that research confirms that children's participation in the larger community is one of the strongest indicators of increased self-esteem and self-confidence? Without a doubt, when you help your daughter connect with the rest of the world—locally and globally—in ways that interest her these experiences will have a direct and positive impact on her confidence and self-esteem. Going out into the world broadens her interests, exposes her to new ideas, and deepens her expertise in a variety of areas. By expanding her horizons she will be able to put into practice some of her own values while she learns citizenship and self-reliance. Encourage her to move out into the world on her own and take advantage of the opportunities that exist away from home.

Developing social consciousness can begin at any age. Your daughter can learn a wide variety of lessons in every activity in which she participates. For example, if she spends a weekend volunteering on a park clean-up crew she is learning about the environment, about cooperation, and about being a team member. She then has the satisfaction of a well-spent day and the sheer delight of tangible results. If she takes swimming lessons, she develops confidence in her body. She will enjoy hours of pleasure in the water with her friends and you won't have to worry when she goes to summer camp!

Helping your daughter connect with the larger community takes time and energy but the rewards are a joy to behold. She will develop a sensitivity to world and community issues as she engages in activities that expand her mind and strengthen her body. Participation can pique her curiosity as well as teach her lessons of commitment and stick-to-itiveness.

She may have her own ideas of activities to get involved in so check with her first. However, most young kids do not know what delicious opportunities are available. As a parent you can be on the lookout and scout out opportunities for her.

Think and plan ahead. Be sure not to overstuff your daughter's schedule. Kids have an inborn right to tons of free time. She does not need to be enrolled in every activity that crosses her path. Free time can be just as educational as a structured event. Collect ideas and work together with your daughter to make interesting and healthy choices that will reflect her interests and your family's schedule and budget. Choose activities that help her build exciting and sturdy bridges to the larger world and give her a real sense of satisfaction. The goal is for her to have experiences that lead her to shout, "Hey, I can do this! Look at me!"

NOTE: An invaluable resource book is *Volunteer USA* by Andrew Carroll (Ballantine, 1991). "A comprehensive guide to worthy causes that need you—from AIDS to the environment to illiteracy—where to find groups, and how you can help."

RIPPLES IN THE POND

People who understand that we all have to live on this planet together who realize the impact each of us has on the rest of the world seem to be able to live with a great deal more enjoyment. These people see diversity as interesting; they approach challenges with energy rather than dread. It takes a certain skill to figure out how we all impact each other. When you help your daughter analyze how events out in the world affect her and her family and how she can be a positive influence for change you help broaden her perspective and build bridges of communication.

My oldest daughter's fifth grade teacher had a great idea. She instructed the students to find a current events newspaper article and write about the ripple effect that the event has on the student, her family, or others. This brainstorming about how an outside event affects your daughter, your family, or other groups of people helps to broaden her awareness of how interconnected we all are. Go ahead and try this ready-made idea. Have your daughter peruse the Sunday paper and find an article of interest. Have her read the article or read it with her. Take a few minutes to explore how the event fits into the bigger picture of life. This discussion can spawn ideas and opinions that reach far beyond the content of the article. A major goal will be to get her thinking about her own importance in the grand scheme of things. How does the world impact her and how would she like to respond? Help her appreciate that she can be affected by others and can in turn have a major impact on the lives of others; even around the world.

Help her analyze what kinds of people and events impact her life for the good and which ones for the bad. How are girls and women affected by this event? Help her pick out underlying themes in articles—themes of prejudice, ignorance, violence, hope, creativity, hunger, fear, or just the hum of life. Life won't feel quite so complicated when she is able to break down the enormity of it into bite-sized pieces. Teach her to look for positive alternatives or solutions to events and figure out how she can be a catalyst for creative change. Ask her how she would solve a problem if she were a world leader.

WORKING VACATIONS

Each spring break my oldest daughter, Rosemary, takes off with her dad for a new destination in the United States that needs a team of hardworking volunteers—volunteers to clean, scrape and paint, build, remodel, haul, or whatever needs to be done. Similar groups may be found all over the country. Her father chaperones a group of college students who give up their spring break vacation to help where help is needed most. Even though Rosemary is only in elementary school, she tags along and becomes a full-fledged volunteer worker. She learns invaluable lessons in living by becoming a part of these work teams. After pondering her latest trip and writing an article about her experience she noted, "I found that you should be glad that you have what you have and that you have a lot more than some other people. I learned more about what other people don't have. The two trips that I took made me realize that it isn't what you have, it's the people that love and care about you." Coincidentally, the news media heard about this particular spring break project and ABC's "Good Morning America" taped the students for national television. What a great way to give a girl the message that she can be noticed in a positive way!

When your daughter uses her own physical energy to bring hope to others less fortunate she is filled with a deep satisfaction of time well spent and a job well done. Your daughter can sign up for even small, local projects and experience the same exhilaration. She can join a work group through the park and recreation system, community projects, church groups and social service organizations. She can even do one-day projects. In fact, the whole family can participate by sharing time and energy serving turkey dinners to the homeless, delivering Christmas gifts and food to someone with AIDS, or helping at the food shelves. Seize any opportunity to help your daughter develop a heart, a deeper sense of compassion for the plight of others, and a core-building social conscience.

It's easy to look the other way, to be too self-absorbed or to be just too plain busy to give much thought to what else needs to be done in the world. Teach your daughter early to see the needs of others and respond with nonjudgmental action. She need not turn into mush or become a glorified caretaker to be effectively compassionate. She can learn through hands-on experiences that she personally can do something that makes a difference in someone else's life.

Step one: Pick an area that your family is interested in funneling some energy. Let your daughter be part of the choice process. Go to the library to get a book on volunteering. Or call your local organizations and find out who needs what when.

Step two: Sign up!

Step three: Do it! Follow through! Commit!

Step four: Recruit others to join her. Encourage her to share her experiences and broaden the ranks of volunteers. Your daughter's enthusiasm and dedication can touch the lives of her friends as well, as she includes them in her goals and activities.

PERFORMING IN PUBLIC

Remember the first time your daughter got up with her preschool class and sang some funny little song with hand motions? There you were, with a silly grin on your face and a video camera in hand, mesmerized by how cute, funny, and totally out-of-tune they were. How sweet it was to be a parent at that moment.

As your daughter gets older she will be faced with many opportunities to perform in public. They won't be quite as easy for her as that first endearing group performance. Initially, performing in public can be downright nerve-racking, but it becomes easier over time and eventually is just plain fun! Helping your daughter get up in front of a group of people to do just about anything is a great confidence booster. Whether it's a piano recital, a swim meet, a baseball game, a dance performance, the science fair, or a spoken presentation, she needs the experience of producing and performing her skills, followed by appreciation and applause. The world is becoming increasingly competitive; she will more than likely need to market herself and her talents as she gets older. Learning to stand up and be noticed comfortably is no longer just a nice idea, it's becoming downright necessary.

The younger she starts, the easier it will be for her in the long run. When she joins a team sport, dance group, or any group activity that culminates in some type of performance or display she eases into this idea of showing off her abilities. It's a lot less scary if everyone else is up there with her. Auditioning for something is more difficult than joining a group with an open door policy. Joining a dance group, for instance, that regularly performs in public places is a great way to get her used to people watching her. Playing a sport is great because she will get the kick of winning, learn the coping skills of losing, and experience the ups and downs of competition. It's good for her to struggle and test her skill and strength against other girls her age. Let her get out there and stretch herself. Let her figure out how her body responds to a variety of physical activities. How does it feel to go on stage? How does it feel to skid unceremoniously into second base? How does she handle stage fright, butterflies, and adrenaline?

Parents may need to move past the natural reaction of grinning ear to ear because she looks so "cute." What she needs help with is learning how to feel confident and capable. Helping her practice ahead of time (a million times) is one of the best confidence builders. This is a major time-consuming task for parents but it pays off in the end. It gives her an opportunity to blow it many times and figure out how to fix the problems as well as get herself out of a variety of mess ups. Teaching her to plow ahead, especially when she gets off track, shows her how to handle the dilemma of "dropping the ball" in public and gives her permission to pick herself up, brush herself off, and keep going; even in front of the crowds.

And when it's all over—whether she won or lost, performed perfectly or stumbled—genuinely praise her. Be the first to congratulate her. Don't snow her with sugar. Instead fill her with messages of how proud you are of her courage, her talents, her gutsiness. Frame her picture or award. Display her project on the living room table. Surround her with the fruits of her achievements. Papering her bedroom walls with her pictures and the articles of her successes and attempts at success are great indirect confidence-builders. Seeing proof of herself out in the world helps her mold her sense of identity.

A Connoisseur of Ethnic Foods

Picky eaters are missing out on one of the most delightful aspects of life. Great food! You don't have to be a world class cook or even like cooking for your daughter to become a world citizen in the field of culinary arts. In fact a friend of mine, Beth Halbrook, laughingly says that she keeps her daughters in line by threatening to cook if they don't behave. When you teach your daughter to be flexible and appreciate a wide variety of food you open up a world of travel and personal enjoyment. I am not saying girls have to like to cook. Not at all. I am suggesting that girls learn to open their fields of experience to include interesting dishes and traditional foods from around the world. It will open a window of opportunity for her to get acquainted with other cultures and people. It will provide her a depth of experience into families other than her own. Other people, countries, and religions offer a wealth of opportunity for her to taste life!

Begin in your own home. Decide what to fix for meals and serve only that. Girls will learn to eat whatever is on the table. Stop assuming they will only eat hot dogs and the like. Don't cater to their finicky demands. Serve a variety of interesting foods. If you start fixing a wide variety and serve new and unusual foods from day one it is a lot easier—she will eat almost all foods. If you're starting later in her life, begin easing in new foods each week. Don't back down or give in to her only having in-the-rut peanut butter sandwiches. Of course everyone has their preferences, but being exposed to a wide variety will increase her foods of choice. If you restrict her food world to hot dogs and macaroni and cheese, then that's all she will come to enjoy. Teach her the beauty of fresh peaches, acorn squash, sautéed mushrooms. If this is new to you, all the better. Model to her how to expand her eating repertoire.

Even parents don't have to enjoy every food, but having an experimental food at least once a week is teaching her to broaden her world of food. Tasting food outside her narrow box will be an interesting experience filled with laughter and strange faces, not a chore. One small benefit is that other parents will love you. Your daughter will eat whatever the other family serves for dinner on those "eating over" nights. Food is a wonderful point of connection among people. It is one of the greatest gathering points available to us. It can be a welcoming, interesting, and nurturing artform. Go ahead and be daring.

You could even designate some weekend afternoons here and there to have a family cooking day. Your daughter can be three or thirteen and still derive a great deal of fun and pleasure if your whole family makes this an event. Pick a country or an exotic-looking recipe, get the groceries, and go for it! And be sure you sit down together and eat as a family. Eating dinner together may be terribly old fashioned but strong and solid bonds form during those hours a family shares dinner. Dinnertime is also a perfect time to put into practice many of the discussion ideas this book advocates. Don't lose this precious and irreplaceable time. Every family is busy. Every night may not work for growing girls. But designate as many nights as possible as absolute family dinnertime. Teach her the importance of families setting a priority of being together. Model for her the ability to find time to be together to eat as a family (with no TV). How else will she learn it? Show her how to experiment with food; include everything in her diet. She can then make healthy and responsible choices for herself as an adult woman.

You can also visit ethnic restaurants and community gatherings for new taste treats. Attend traditional dinners and holiday gatherings for a variety of ethnic groups, cultures and religions. Walk on the wild side and try Korean Kim Chi. This stuff will grow hair on your chest and will have everyone laughing hysterically the first time they try it. Explore your city and try foods indigenous to the Scandinavians, the Jewish, the Africans. Try authentic Greek, Southeast Asian, Lebanese. Visit one completely new-to-you ethnic restaurant each month or attend authentic dinners put on by community groups. These dinners are particularly popular around holidays for that country. Read the paper, especially the small neighborhood papers. Look for posted flyers. Contact churches, community centers, and private cultural organizations. They love newcomers and the price is almost always very affordable, even for a meal for a whole family.

Why food? Because it draws us all together. We all eat. We all can share our table with others. Teach her to welcome others into her home. Teach her to share. Teach her to be gracious, daring, social, and flexible. These are traits that will help her truly become a connoisseur of fine, original food; she will become a woman of the world.

COMMITTEES THAT CARE

Most schools have a student council where one kid from each classroom is voted to serve as a representative. There's nothing wrong with this, but do you know who the member is from your daughter's classroom? Is it the same popular kid, voted in year after year? When schools have only one vehicle for contributing time and energy, the same kids get picked over and over. The classroom voting structure can become a mindless mass of hands going up to support only one, leaving everyone else with nothing to do.

Then there are schools and organizations that form a variety of committees covering a host of topics. Your daughter can sign up for committees that pique her interest and fit her schedule. Better yet, your daughter could initiate the formation of these committees!

Committees that Care can be initiated anywhere your daughter belongs to a cohesive group. She could be in charge of rallying support and organizing groups of other kids to put out positive energy. Perhaps she could introduce a series of committees that address the social issues and needs of others. The entire fifth grade could be in charge of a used clothing drive. The eighth grade could organize a canned food collection. The kindergartners could collect mittens, scarves, and hats from friends and relatives. Age is not a factor. Girls can be taught at any age to be compassionate and caring with a focused purpose and end result. Simply feeling bad about those in her world who are struggling and hurting doesn't bring any sense of accomplishment. Taking directed action to alleviate even a small piece of the problem with a creative, specific solution is going to bring her a deep sense of inner satisfaction. And everyone can be included!

POLITICAL AWARENESS

Girls and women, young and old can make their voices heard throughout the land by being in touch politically. You or your daughter do not have to be avid political followers to be involved and heard. Whether it's election time or not, try to stay on top of the issues being debated. Around election time your daughter will be exposed to candidates and issues at school as part of her current events studies. The rest of the time, it will be up to you to educate and involve your daughter in the political process. Whether you passionately love the political process or can barely tolerate elected officials, the fact remains that laws are made and changed through this system: laws that affect your daughter and women everywhere; laws that affect her educational process, her work environment, her physical safety, and her basic freedoms. Decisions are made regarding war and peace, social programs, human rights. Individuals and groups continually challenge and define the core meaning of the Constitution. It's interesting stuff for your daughter to get her hands and voice around.

Understanding the process

Your daughter will probably learn the basic political structure and process at school. It is still a good idea to discuss at home who's who and how the system works. Use daily news articles to generate your own kitchen table debates. The more family members are involved the better. It keeps things lively and opinionated. Family members can disagree and have spirited debates and don't have to adhere to any strict political party line. Work with your daughter to explain how various topics, issues, and laws are being handled through the governing bodies. Take current, hot topics and ask your daughter what she thinks. Find out her opinion on the current topics of interest and concern of your state or the entire nation. Discuss with her how the government deals with the issues and how they make laws. Pick her political brain, not to bring her around to your way of thinking, but to help her strengthen her own powers of analysis and political voice.

In addition to laws and topics of national interest and concern, discuss other legal matters—matters such as important court cases going on locally and nationally. Help her follow the cases as presented by the prosecution and the defense. What does she think of the evidence? What does she think of the way the case is being tried? What might she do if she were involved?

Meeting candidates and elected officials

It's very easy to meet or at least hear political candidates and officials. During campaign time take your daughter to events where the candidates are speaking. Let her see what it's like to be involved in the process. Let her hear for herself what the candidate has to say. You can go in person or watch speeches or debates on television. If she's quite young, paraphrase the message for her and ask her what she thinks of what the candidate is saying. Is the candidate saying anything pertaining to women or women's issues? Educational issues? Employment issues? Be sure to tell your daughter. She has a right to know, even if she's not old enough to vote. She can still contact this candidate with her opinion!

Postelection she can visit the offices of officials, the capitol buildings, the libraries, and any other building that houses lawmakers. Familiarize her with where it all takes place. Urge her school to take field trips there, if none have been planned. Volunteer to go along.

Voicing her opinion

Here's the fun part: Teach her how to establish and voice her own political opinion. Try not to impose your own opinion on her. Political freedom is such a basic right—one that she should experience in her own home. Here is another opportunity to write, write, write, to the powers that be. It's especially important for her to write postelection or if a major issue is under debate. Help her sort out her thoughts and opinions. Use dinner conversations to help her hone her ideas. Sharpen her thoughts through friendly but rigorous discussion. Don't corner or entrap her. Remember her cognitive (thinking) skills are not as developed as an adult's. Her skills are less refined, but interesting discussions will motivate her to think clearly. When she knows what she wants to say to an elected official, turn on the computer or get out the pencil and paper and let her go to work. Don't direct her thoughts or words, let her write the letter on her own. Praise her for her energy and interest in voicing her opinion. Be sure to mail the letter—don't let it wither on the kitchen counter. Whether she writes to the President of the United States or a school board member she will usually get a response.

As she reviews the issues in the paper or on the news, urge to her write to the official involved. Write to the county commissioners, the school board members, park board members, the mayor, the governor, and state and federal senators and representatives. Your daughter can also call her elected officials to leave her message verbally or she can visit their local offices to leave her message.

Boards of Trustees

Boards of Trustees are another interesting place for her to make her opinion known. If there is a school, corporation, church or any other organization that is involved in an issue that concerns or affects your daughter encourage her to write or call the board member. After all, these are the people behind the decisions in major organizations that may involve your daughter. Their response (or lack thereof) will be good information to her about decisions that affect her daily life.

School project

Perhaps she could apply for extra credit at school for a project that involves contacting elected officials. Writing thirty letters to elected officials, board members, or heads of organizations, then compiling them with the responses might make a good current events project. It's worth a try; it will keep your daughter interested and committed in the world that surrounds her.

Madame President

Sometime, some woman is going to become the first woman President of the United States of America. Why not your daughter? Plant the seed of possibility now, while she has time to think and plan. Clearly give her the message that she can become President. At some point during elementary school, usually while studying the Presidents, most girls stop, think and ask, "Is there some law that says only men can become President?" The answer of course is "No." And yet, why haven't there been any? When will there be?

What would your daughter like to do about it?

HONORING MOTHER NATURE

Think about the weather in your environment. Do you have wild and woolly days, blizzards, droughts, heat waves, glorious fall foliage? Are spring mornings pristine with delicate wildflowers, returning perennials and the smell of the earth warming itself up? Do you have thunderstorms, ice and snow, lush summer flower gardens, or bountiful fall harvests? Do the seasons change right on schedule and bring a fresh new batch of weather, or is it hard to detect one season from another?

Everyone has a place that truly feels like home. It really doesn't matter if it's New York City or a small Iowa farm. It's where you and your daughter have nestled. It's home.

Wherever you live, encourage your daughter to get to know her most prominent neighbor, Mother Nature. Living simply enough to allow time outdoors teaches your daughter to respect and walk gently and mindfully on the Earth. It's the only one we've got, let's not blow it. Teaching your daughter to be ecologically minded will put her in the company of others who care about preserving our natural resources and the Earth itself. We cannot abandon our responsibility to protect this gift that has been loaned to us for our daily use.

Your daughter may or may not be an outdoorsy girl. She can still learn to communicate and make friends with nature. She doesn't have to dig for worms to appreciate the soil. Here are some ideas to put her in touch with nature.

Plant a tree in her honor

Let this be her tree. Give it to her as a gift with the understanding that she is responsible for its well-being. Teach her to water it, watch for and treat diseases or bugs, and prune it. Buy her a small book about trees that includes the care and maintenance of her type of tree. Take a picture each year of her standing next to her tree. Keep the photos in a special, small, hand-sized picture album. Over time she may draw pictures of her tree or write a poem or short story about it to add to her album. Trees take a long time to grow, but then so do girls. It's a rather perfect combination. If you don't own any land, you can donate trees to many parks, landscape arboretums, or organizations that treasure heritage and nature.

Recycle

Everybody does it. It's "in." Put her in charge of keeping the recycling bin in order. She can be the one to put out fresh collection bags each week and remind the family to recycle rather than throw out plastic, paper, glass, and aluminum. Suggest that she ask her teacher about visiting a recycling center to see the mammoth piles of recycling material. Try to avoid excessive packaging and materials that cannot be recycled. If she goes with you to the grocery store, have her check the bottoms on containers to look for the recycling symbol.

Start a garden

It can be a window box or a full-sized extravaganza of a garden. Include her in choosing plants and seeds, preparing the soil, planting, and maintenance. Give her a plot or single pot of her own to plant and tend. Picking her own flowers or vegetables is a deeply satisfying experience. If you have space, plant some perennials; when the time comes you can split them and give them to her when she has room to start her own garden at her own place.

Plan family outings to state or national parks

Do a little preparation and bring along guidebooks for trees and wildflowers. Teach her to be a girl knowledgeable about plants and animals. This is particularly enjoyable if you live in a state with changing seasons; you can return to the same parks and see the cycles of change. As she learns to watch for change, she can be taught to respect the cycle of life—the necessary changes for growth and rest.

Teach her to respect the environment

Role-model your concern by putting action to your words. Never do the things you know are destructive to the earth. Teach her that small is beautiful—that she should not to hog the gifts the Earth gives her.

Adorn her room with nature's gifts

Let her decorate her room with fresh flowers from the garden, a pumpkin she carved herself, pine boughs in winter, a bowl of acorns in the fall. Let her try to grow moss and tiny plants in a terrarium. Put a bouquet of dried leaves in a bottle. Let her collect seashells discarded by their previous occupants, pieces of driftwood, and fungus. Show her how to make colored sand designs in a jar.

Give her a subscription to a nature magazine

Put in her hands an interesting magazine that teaches about the Earth. Gear it to her age and sit down and page through it with her. Encourage her to try some of the experiments it describes. Discuss with her the articles that describe the tragic misuse of the Earth for which humans are responsible. Urge her to write to the editor with her ideas and concerns.

Introduce her to activist organizations

You don't have to join to get information from numerous organizations that are steadily working to preserve the Earth. Organizations such as The National Wildlife Foundation, The Izak Walton League, and Greenpeace. You don't have to agree with their entire philosophy to use their literature to teach and sensitize your daughter.

Attend camps with an environmental focus

Many school districts now include an overnight environmental camping experience as part of the curriculum. You and your daughter could consider approaching her school if this is not already happening. In addition, she could attend this kind of a camp during summer vacation. She will learn a great deal in a few days and nights of directed study.

Watch nature programs on TV

Your daughter may be captivated by a program on bugs or antelopes. She can become a wealth of information about plants and animals.

LEARNING CONFLICT-
RESOLUTION SKILLS

If you are like many parents, you realize, usually right in the middle of a big mess, that you are not very familiar with conflict-resolution skills. You are not alone. You weren't born with these skills. They have to be learned. So do not expect yourself to know how to handle every conflict right off the bat.

As you begin to teach your daughter communication and conflict-resolution skills, keep in mind that these skills are absolutely not about teaching her to be a doormat or a wimp! Negotiation is very different from manipulation. Having good manners and respectful behavior is different from acting like a mouse. As you teach your daughter interpersonal skills, you are opening gigantic doors and windows of opportunity that will help her throughout her life. This is particularly important because everything in society has turned upside down; nothing is guaranteed anymore. As girls become women they will emerge into a highly complex and competitive world of constant change. Girls need to know how to negotiate their way through the three big "C"s: Change, Conflict, and Crisis.

A multitude of opportunities are available to teach your daughter vital negotiating skills that leave her feeling satisfied and respected in her interactions. She must learn how to talk in a way that will cause others to take her seriously and hear what she has to say or she will be constantly frustrated, misunderstood, and shut out. Being mealy-mouthed, vague, whiny, or just plain obnoxious is not going to help build her confidence. In fact, just the opposite is needed. When she knows the words to say and the demeanor to present when dealing with conflict or crisis she enables others to settle down long enough to hear what she has to say. She can begin at any age to learn how to clearly, firmly, and definitively state what she means in a way that builds bridges of communication. Society still expects girls to be less aggressive and less assertive than boys. If she learns how to be aggressive and assertive in a proactive way she can be on the cutting edge of creative change.

It is also important to teach her how to leave negative situations and stop banging her head against the wall. She can learn the importance of cutting her losses and getting on with her life when she encounters a bad situation or a relationship that is doomed to fail or to hurt her. As she learns these diplomatic, communication skills, she will develop the satisfaction of knowing that she chose the higher road for herself and has been the best person she could possibly be in a difficult, conflicted world.

PERSONAL RESPONSIBILITY FOR THE YOUNGER SET

You know the mornings. The school bus is roaring toward your corner and your cherub is hanging out in her room half in, half out of her pajamas humming to herself and dinging around with something or other she has spied on top of her dresser. Or, you are frantically trying to get everyone out the door because you need to get somewhere on time and the cooperation level is registering zero. Or, you are concentrating on one child who is working on a project and you have instructed your little one to get her teeth brushed and

jammies on. Fifteen minutes later, she has not even begun her bedtime routine. It is as if you never spoke. You are invisible. Face it,
you have been totally tuned out by a shrimp.

Sometimes these daily frustrations roll off your back. On other
days they add up until you lose it and start screaming like a crazy
person. But instead of your daughter responding with improved
behavior she just looks at you like you are from another planet. At
this point you:

    a) pack your bags and leave home permanently
    b) tell your daughter she will be spending the rest of her life in "time-
       out"
    c) wonder why on earth you ever decided to have children
    d) try the button jar of happiness

We have all tried taking away privileges after the fact. After your
daughter does something dreadful, you come up with "the punishment." This is completely appropriate. Sometimes. However, the
button jar strategy helps you set out in advance a clear statement of
what you expect from your daughter. If (and only if) these expectations are met does your daughter earn X number of reward buttons. It works quite simply. You create a simple, easy-to-follow chart
ahead of time listing each expectation and how many buttons she
earns for meeting each one. You also decide how many buttons
equal each reward. Keep the Button Jar only for positives. Never
use it to take away buttons or privileges. Also, it is important that
the earned rewards be enticing to her and not just something you
would like. Clearly identifying your basic expectations ahead of
time avoids a myriad of misunderstandings and nasty interactions.
Rewarding her for meeting expectations makes everyone happy—
you get the desired behavior, she gets the goodie.

Buttons are particularly fun. You can always find interesting
ones from relatives, garage sales, or antiques sales. Many little girls
are quite fascinated with them, which makes them perfect to use.
Not only does she earn her reward buttons but she also gets the

added bonus of picking her favorite button. These buttons can be placed in a see-through jar on her bookshelf until she earns enough to "purchase" something neat. You can choose whatever medium works for you, marbles, coins, or exotic pebbles. Candy does not work, however, because it is rotten for her teeth and any self-respecting kid worth her salt is going to scarf it down the second you are not looking! Have fun dreaming up rewards and ideas with your daughter.

SOLUTION-FOCUSED LISTENING
A THUMBNAIL SKETCH

Down-home listening

When a parent listens—really listens to a daughter—minor miracles begin to unfold. Oftentimes your method and style of interacting with your daughter can truly make the difference between her staying stuck, mad, confused, frustrated, and unclear how to proceed and her being able to smooth the way toward positive, workable solutions. It doesn't require fancy words or techniques, but it does take concentration and a commitment on your part. A parent who listens is a blessing for a daughter to thrive on. A judgmental, know-it-all parent does massive damage by shutting down the vital lines of communication between parent and daughter. If the latter is your style, over time your daughter won't talk to you anymore because she doesn't feel you listen or understand. Soon you will be left out of the "communication loop"; there is no colder place for a concerned parent to be. Your daughter needs a clear, impartial ear to help her sort out life. The glory of it all is that developing good—no, great—listening skills takes intense commitment, time, and focused energy but it's amazingly simple to do! The benefits you will reap go beyond your wildest dreams. Imagine your daughter talking to you about herself and her life, all through elementary, middle, and high school. What could be better?

Tangled relationships

Most of your daughter's crises will be relationship-oriented. She will be hurt and angered by someone at school—a classmate, friend, or teacher. Siblings and boyfriends are another prime source of relationship disasters, blow-ups, and general agony for a growing girl. Along with her problem, she may experience physical symptoms. Your daughter may complain of headaches, stomachaches, feeling dizzy, generalized aches and pains, difficulty breathing or relaxing, crying, or odd complaints of one kind or other. Often this is simply her body responding to insecurity, fear, and general upset. When she feels a situation is out of control her body may take over and help her slow down or shut down, so to speak. Her body may be saying, "get out of here, hide under the covers, this is too overwhelming!" Anxiety is the body's way of calling "time out! I can't handle this!"

Creating the listening environment

Helping your daughter can be as close and easy as one good listening session away. A few simple steps will start the process of unraveling the problem and moving toward a hopeful, positive outcome.

Let her vent while you quietly listen
To put it another way, be quiet. Join her in her moment. Bite your tongue, button your lip, freeze your urge to interrupt, control your overwhelming desire to talk, do whatever you have to do to join and connect with her by quietly listening, taking in every word, feeling, nuance, and body message she is giving to you. Don't jump in with ideas or solutions. Don't minimize what she is saying by rushing in with suggestions. Let her say everything she needs to say. She may cry or be angry or blame everyone else. For now, let her. Don't cut her off. If you do, she will not feel understood and you will lose her right from the beginning. Let it be safe for her to tell you her problem.

Let her define the problem

Let her state in her own words what she thinks is the problem or conflict. Don't try to put words in her mouth or change how she is seeing or describing the situation. Don't try to talk her out of the problem or imply that it isn't even a problem at all. Relate back to her what you hear her saying the problem is, but don't change the words or meaning around to fit your perspective.

Ask the right questions and assure her of your support

Prove to her that you are there for her. Show her your best parenting skills. Be an expert at parenting but mainly be an expert at asking all the right questions. Ask all the really good questions and then listen, listen, listen. Examples of questions are:

> "Tell me what happened, I really want to hear and I have lots of time to listen."
> "And then what happened after that?"
> "Help me understand."
> "How did you feel when it happened? Did you cry? Did you get really angry?"
> "How are you feeling now? You look so sad, (mad, upset, worried. . .)."
> "Are your feelings hurt?"
> "Are you afraid this can't be fixed?"

Follow your questions with a few statements of assurance. "Normalize" the problem or situation for her, but be careful not to discount her and her feelings. Assure her and comfort her. Never shame or embarrass her. Never make her regret she told you her problem. Let her know she's not alone and that others have experienced similar troubles in their lives, but again, be cautious about making light of her deep feelings. You can assure her that you will be there to help and will continue to listen and puzzle this out with her no matter how long it takes. Ask her if it would be okay if you held her or gave her a hug. If so, continue to rub her back or stroke her hand as she continues talking. The physical contact can be very comforting, but if she moves away, let her go.

Create hope

Slowly and carefully begin to help her reframe the problem in a manageable light. If she's still venting, so be it. Don't rush her. She may be good and upset and may need additional time to blow. Moving in too quickly with attempts to move ahead and change the situation usually meet with flat-out resistance and the conversation falls apart. Once again, you may simply lose her if you move too quickly. Timing is everything. Timing is a skill that can be learned by anyone. It's a tremendous skill that is worth it's weight in gold. Nudge and challenge. Never push and shove.

Have her think about similar situations in her life. Whether she's five or sixteen, she has probably experienced something like this before. She has probably had these feelings before. Help her think about those times. Suggest she recall how she solved that problem.

Own your own words

Relate back to her what you hear her saying. If you have something to say, make "I" statements: "I think . . . ," "I feel . . . ," "I heard you say . . . ," "I wonder if . . . ." That way you won't be putting words in her mouth or talking on her behalf. You'll be talking only for yourself.

Create motivation for her to change

Begin to talk with her about ways to solve this dilemma. Assure her you understand that she may not think it's fixable, but that you would like her to give it a try and see if there might be some options. Urge her to decide on the next step herself. Challenge her to come up with a few options. Let her prove to herself that she does have good ideas and options at her disposal. Help her think of some reasons to attempt to change and/or fix this mess. What might be some benefits to her in solving this?

Is she in the doghouse at school or with others?

Perhaps her problem includes being in trouble with others. Or, even if she's not technically in trouble, maybe her part in the problem is big enough to warrant a closer inspection by you. If so, try not to become defensive. Much as any parent would like it to be, the truth of the matter is that no one's daughter is a perfect little darling all the time. Perhaps your daughter was part (even a big part) of the problem. It does not mean by any stretch of the imagination that you are a bad parent. It just means your daughter is struggling to learn a lesson in life and she doesn't have it down pat yet. She could really use your help with learning the lesson far more than she needs you to rush to her defense with excuses for her and accusations of others. Role-model for her how to lower defenses and approach her teacher or coach with an open mind and a willingness to understand the problem so that it can be tackled and resolved.

If you think and react to the problem only from your own emotional state, you will be paralyzed by your misguided loyalty and will be virtually no help to her in finding positive solutions. Approach her teacher with honest questions and be willing to listen to the answers. Does your daughter need help with something? Does she need guidance in getting along with others? If so, help her learn these basic life skills. If you miss these day-to-day opportunities, she may never learn what she needs to and will continue to struggle with relationships throughout her life. Don't be too quick to side with your daughter completely or to point blaming fingers at the other party. This is not about taking sides. It's about your daughter learning to live cooperatively, problem-solving situations creatively as they arise. It's not someone else's fault that your daughter hit someone, doesn't become a star player, chose not to complete her assignment, or turned into a bossy cow with her work group. Again, it's not about finding fault, it's about proactively finding solutions and new ways of meeting these issues head-on. Don't deprive her of learning these vital lessons.

When tough situations come up for your daughter, be the best parent you can be. Listen with every ounce of your being, ask her thoughtful, compassionate questions, and assure her you will be there to support and help her. Let her define the problem; when she's ready, be there to help her move ahead toward creative change and solutions. If she's part of the problem, help her by not blaming others but by supporting her to make positive changes in her own behavior.

THE OPEN-MINDED GIRL

Is there is anything so ugly as prejudice and bigotry—statements and beliefs perpetuated out of ignorance; racial and sexual prejudice born out of fear; and pathetic attempts to raise up oneself by denigrating another who appears different? Snickering at differences isn't humor, it's a sign of ignorance. The goal of wisdom and maturity can be reached in ourselves and our daughters through open minds and hearts to encompass other races, religions, creeds, lifestyles, values, and beliefs.

Growing girls can be both the focus of this bigotry and the bearers of their own prejudices. Teaching tolerance can be a difficult task for parents who have to grapple with their own ingrained prejudices. We all suffer from this affliction to one extent or another. We all like to think we are open-minded. Unfortunately, a lot of the time we're not. We don't mean to hurt, we are just blind. It's hard to be opened-minded when other people do things we think are wrong. Are parents to advocate and teach their daughters to just live and let live, that there is no right or wrong? No. But the tricky part is that what might be right for one person can be very wrong for another. Ultimately, we all have to arrive at our own definition of truth. Perhaps that is the place to start. Help her define and carve out her own sense of personal truth. Let her grapple with the gray areas, the fuzzy, undefined parts of life. Don't rush in and tell her what to think.

105

Different or disenfranchised?

People who are born looking different from us and people who later become disenfranchised can become the focus of our bigotry. People who are disenfranchised have been dealt a harsh blow by life by being caught in the endless traps of poverty and all of its manifestations. They don't have access to all the opportunities for good living your daughter has. They experience life in poverty, sickness, dysfunctional surroundings, and anger. It is important to teach your daughter tolerance of differences and compassion for people whose lives are deprived of basic opportunities for growth and happiness.

Learning tolerance

First off let's be clear about what tolerance and acceptance of others are and are not. Most important—it does not mean that you have to agree or choose that lifestyle for yourself. It does mean allowing others to make choices or live differently than you do without standing in judgment of them. All of us are responsible only for our own lives. No one is responsible for anyone else's life; therefore no one has the right to stand in judgment of other people. Others are born into their own families, races, religions, and lifestyles—just like us, only different.

Teaching young girls tolerance and acceptance is an extraordinary gift. Why? Because the world is full to bursting with other people, each one unique. If your daughter can learn to celebrate and derive great enjoyment from these differences, what a welcome addition she will be to any gathering or group. She can be free to visit, travel, work, or be in relationships with a diverse and fascinating mix of people. What fun!

Who, what, when, where, and how?

An endless supply of fun and interesting ways to enlighten our minds exists for all of us. Learning tolerance and acceptance of others doesn't have to be a grueling task; it can bring great joy and friendship along the way.

Visit the community centers of various ethnic groups
Attend some of their native, cultural programs and feasts. Learn about the symbols and traditions of other races and nationalities.

Consider taking in a foreign exchange student
This is a huge commitment but the rewards are astounding. Consider having your daughter be a foreign exchange student as part of her high school education.

Neighborhood meetings
Bring your daughter to neighborhood meetings outside your own neighborhood. Learn about the issues and concerns of other groups of people outside your own sphere. What are the priorities and issues being discussed in other parts of your city?

Cultural diversity work groups
Volunteer for or start a cultural diversity work group in your daughter's school. Bring to light issues of intolerance and brainstorm how to find creative solutions to open up young minds.

Books
Read autobiographies of people of other races, religions and lifestyles.

Presentations
Attend presentations by people culturally different from you and your family.

Discuss the topic of cultural diversity at home
Bring together everyone's opinion. Debate the issues. Call each other on prejudicial remarks.

Find resources to answer honest questions

A great deal of prejudice is founded in a lack of basic knowledge. The unknown is scary; many times we make things up that aren't even true about other groups of people.

Diversity training

Bring to your daughter's attention the positive, creative activities of a diverse group of people. Expand your daughter's focus out far beyond her immediate family and neighborhood.

Soul-search your own heart

Shine a spotlight on all your own prejudices and yes, bigotries. If you are willing to acknowledge and change them you need not be ashamed of them. Admit which groups of people frighten you, disgust you, or make you bitter and angry. Think long and hard about your prejudices. Where do they come from? Are they just old worn-out messages you heard from your parents growing up? Are you afraid "those people" will take something away from you or hurt you? Are you angry because you feel they aren't "decent" people? If you are willing to bring your intolerance to light, figure out where it came from and what purpose it is serving in your life now you can release and heal it. If you choose not to, you will remain stuck in the dark. If you choose to heal yourself you will become one more shining light in this sometimes dark, troubled, and angry world.

Practicing compassion

Volunteer to serve at a homeless shelter

Introduce the people staying there to your daughter. Let her meet them and talk to them firsthand. Teach her to open her hands and heart to real, individual people, caught in the nightmare of homelessness. Move beyond nameless, faceless masses.

Charity

Support her to save a portion of her money on a regular basis to be given to organizations of her choice. (See chapter 8.) Point out news articles or information about charitable organizations that really roll up their sleeves and work hard to help those struggling and in need.

Teach her to see the needs of others

Sometimes the sadness and need of others is so overwhelming she doesn't know where to begin. Begin one by one with individual situations. Show her how to help even one person.

Educate her to the needs of others

Sensitize her to the devastating effects of poverty and AIDS. Help her to understand with compassion the anguish of others who are struggling with heroic courage to stay alive. Teach her not to judge but to reach out.

Teach her to ask for help when she needs it

Show her how to not get caught up in the web of pride to the extent that she stumbles along and refuses to ask for what she needs for herself.

Show your daughter how to be a light in this world—to never add to the darkness of ignorance, intolerance, and bigotry.

HALT GIRLS BASHING GIRLS

It's appalling to hear girls bashing each other with such abandon. They can really get into it, saying things to each other that make your hair stand on end. One has to wonder why they are so vicious with each other. They can rip into each other with such a vengeance that it's amazing that either one has a shred of self-esteem or confidence left. They rag on each other about how the other looks, smells, dresses, combs her hair, studies, keeps her room, chooses boyfriends, eats, grooms, and spends time in the bathroom—every conceivable personality trait and characteristic they can think of. They make Cinderella's step-sisters, Anastasia and Driscilla, look like fairy godsisters.

Where is their sense of sisterhood? Bonding? Why the obvious disregard for another girl? Perhaps is is because they are young girls, not yet versed in the collective issues that women face. These are girls just struggling to get along; they sometimes bash someone else to feel better about themselves and elevate their own faltering esteem and confidence. It doesn't help to lecture them on the importance of staying connected as girls and women. They aren't at that point in their lives. Their struggles are much more immediate and have more to do with immaturity and growing up. Yet with some personalities, the power struggles continue well into adulthood. Many sisters (and brothers) are still verbally duking it out well into their retirement.

Understanding differences

As your daughter grows and matures help her understand the differences between herself and other girls. Help her realize and comprehend that all girls are unique—individuals in their own right. Differences in style and personality are good. Taking pot-shots and having fits over differences is not. You may have to set some limits and boundaries over how much infighting you will allow between your daughter and her siblings or girlfriends. Basic respect and common courtesy can't be thrown out the window permanently as these girls zoom in for the attack.

You may feel that all your hard work to build up each girl's esteem and confidence is completely destroyed after your daughter is involved in one of these seek and destroy missions. It probably is not, although it will have taken quite a beating. This struggle to get on the top of the heap isn't necessarily "character building" but in most cases, the girl survives. In some cases, however, great damage can be done. It is at that point that parents definitely need to

110

get involved. There is no point in being cruel and hurtful to the point of no return. Hateful, bitter words cannot be taken back. Your daughter needs to realize the impact of her words. If she's on the receiving end, it may be time to step in and talk to the teacher or other parent. Your daughter does not deserve to be constantly humiliated and attacked by another girl.

Role-modeling

Parents also need to be aware of any girl- or woman-bashing tendencies that may exist in the family. It may not even be a conscious thing. It may just be the snickers when a girl or woman makes a mistake, or when she sticks her neck out and is thought a fool. It may be derogatory comments about women in general: women drivers, politicians, managers, entertainers. This is not to say that your daughter is being nasty to other girls because she is learning it at home, but it is worth examining.

Techniques

1) Make clear to her you do not tolerate girl bashing. The best way to do this is by proactively not doing it yourself. Model to her respect. If necessary, teach her how to agree to disagree.

2) Separate the girls. Refuse to allow this behavior to continue in your presence. Keeping them close together isn't going to force them to get along. It probably will do just the opposite and keep the fire burning. If they are sharing a bedroom, help them design physical boundaries. They will be more than glad to set up my-side your-side boundaries. This isn't prolonging the battle; it may give them some temporary breathing room.

3) Show your daughter how to speak up for herself—to neither wimp out nor get into it herself. Too often when attacked girls will take one or the other of these routes. Wimping out leaves her feeling bad about herself, hurt, angry, and tearful. If your daughter rolls her eyes and lets the other girl "get away with it" she doesn't make

clear that she will not tolerate this behavior from another girl. The other girl should not get to take over your daughter's world. Having your daughter go on the attack doesn't work either because then the two of them are slinging mud. Everybody ends up in the slime.

Your daughter needs to be clear, confident, and straightforward. Your daughter will need to address overly aggressive girls (or boys) in no uncertain terms, telling them that she will not be treated or spoken to in that way. Demanding respect from a peer can be very difficult. Your daughter may need to enlist the help of an adult. Keep your ear peeled; listen for continued struggles your daughter may be having at school with a particular girl. Step in when necessary. It's okay to involve yourself where you're not wanted when your daughter needs help.

4) Be willing to handle the situation if it's your daughter who's going on the attack. She needs your help if she is overly aggressive and mean to other girls. Help her think through how the other girl might be feeling. Don't demand that she think of how it makes the other girl feel! Talk her through process of thinking about what some of the other girl's feelings might be. Empathy training is something she can use throughout her life, not just this year with this girl. Your daughter may need to learn how to be strong and confident without running over other girls like a freight train.

5) Help your daughter understand her feelings. Whether she's on the giving end, the receiving end, or both, help her process how it makes her feel. If she blows it off and says she doesn't care and her feelings aren't hurt, nudge her to be honest. Her feelings can be an informative guide to her of how to respond in the future.

THE STRAIGHTFORWARD GIRL

Forget being a wishy-washy girl. Let's raise girls to speak up and be clear and straightforward in asking for what they need and want. To this day, so many girls and women take the back seat in silence. They wait and hope that someone will magically know what they are thinking, wanting, or needing. We must teach our daughters that no one can read their minds; they have to speak up and be heard.

Many adult women suffer in silence in relationships and at work. They hope their partner or co-worker will see how they are feeling or what they need. Most of the time, this is not going to happen. The burden of "seeing" and "knowing" what she wants cannot be placed on someone else. It is wonderful when partners and co-workers are sensitive to needs and come forth without being told and do just the right thing. But, more often than not, people are muddling along their own path and can't be expected to know what someone else is thinking or feeling. Girls and women need to work hard to clarify their needs and wants and make them known to those around them. It's not fair to expect others to read minds, nor is it fair to girls and women never to get their needs met.

Speaking up

Learning to speak up is a lifelong process. Every girl has her own personality. Some are shy and soft-spoken, some are boisterous and gregarious, and most are somewhere in between. Teaching your daughter to be straightforward does not mean she should change her personality. She should enhance her style to include clear and honest statements about what she needs and wants from others and life. Teach her to ask direct questions and not to beat around the bush—to learn confidence and not to wimp out.

"I'm Sorry"

Saying "I'm sorry" is often the most profoundly appropriate statement that we can make to another human being. It is an admission of responsibility for an action or word gone awry as well as a plea for forgiveness. The problem only arises when girls and women find themselves virtually apologizing for their very existence. Every time anything goes wrong no matter what the cause or reason, these girls and women apologize. If someone is disturbed or experiences discomfort in any way, these girls say "I'm sorry." After a while, saying "I'm sorry" becomes a habit. Does this "sorry" statement come from low self-esteem? Possibly. Or perhaps it's just a natural, self-effacing response to anything that happens in life. If you have an "I'm sorry" girl at your house, it's time to change her pattern of thinking and repertoire of responses. For example, if something doesn't turn out right, instead of saying "I'm sorry" she could say "Well, that didn't turn out how we planned." If she bumps into someone, she could say a simple "excuse me." If she interrupts someone, she could say "I'll wait my turn." Anything but "I'm sorry." Teach her when it is appropriate to offer a heartfelt apology, but otherwise work to correct a bad habit.

Asking questions

Asking questions is another stickler for many girls. They would rather sit in silence and wonder than speak up and ask a direct question. Perhaps they don't want to look stupid, to be noticed, to take up time, or to be in the spotlight. And so instead of asking the expert they guess or ask their friends. They stay in the shadows and hope they can figure it out on their own so nobody will know that they don't know. This hiding type behavior does not tend to go away with age. It just gets worse and filters its way into all aspects of a woman's life. It becomes hard for her to talk about money, ask for jobs or raises, speak up to her in-laws or boss, or tell her significant other her concerns or what she needs and wants.

Start young to train your daughter to clarify her thoughts and questions. it will provide her ample time to learn this skill before it cements itself into her personality style. Begin right at home. Whether she is four or fourteen insist that she ask her questions directly in a normal tone of voice. Help her to lose the whiny voice and not dance around the issue or question. Don't get into playing the game with her where you are supposed to know or guess what it is she is trying to tell you. Gently but firmly insist that she be straightforward.

This learning process can continue in the school classroom. If she is shy and tends to fade by nature, talk to her teacher(s) and enlist their help to bring her out into the limelight. Even first-graders can be taught bravery by being assigned to bring messages down to the office or to another classroom. Teens can be taught to be honest and upfront when they don't understand an assignment or project. Teachers are not only interested in teaching your daughter academic subjects. If you have a concern about your daughter's social or personality skills, discuss them candidly in a straightforward manner with your daughter's teacher. She or he will probably be a wealth of information on techniques to help your daughter. Never leave her teacher out of anything important in your daughter's development. Teachers have years of training and experience; they seem to have an unending supply of incredibly good and often easy-to-try ideas to help kids and parents deal with a variety of concerns. Besides, your daughter spends so much of her life in school, it's a natural place to practice asking direct questions until she feels comfortable that she knows the next step.

Being straightforward

Being straightforward means your daughter is able to state the facts and her feelings clearly and honestly; she has no need for flinching or shame, she just calls it as she sees it. Being straightforward is different from being obnoxious. Being straightforward is not about cramming her opinion or what she wants down someone else's throat. It certainly is not throwing a fit or having a tantrum. It simply means she is able to describe herself and her needs and wants clearly and succinctly.

Your part is to listen carefully to her. Allow her to experience what it's like to be truly and carefully listened to. It will be easier for her to learn the skill of being straightforward if she is being listened to. Learning this early on in life will save her a tremendous amount of grief and emotional upset as a grown women. So many adult women don't feel listened to. If your daughter learns early, she will know for certain when she is grown whether or not someone is listening to and paying attention to her. She won't have to guess and hope. She will know. So listen well and don't make her feel as though she has to defend herself and her thoughts and feelings to a panel of judges. Just do your best listening and help her express herself as clearly and boldly as she can.

WHAT'S RIGHT WITH THIS PICTURE?

Isn't it great to be around positive people—people who are able to see creative solutions and who refuse to be squashed by disappointments and setbacks? Teach your daughter to look at life and see what's right. This certainly does not mean teaching her to turn her back on the struggles of life. Nor does it mean turning her into a Pollyanna. Helping her be in touch with her own feelings and the realities of life does not exclude her from reframing them into a positive, resourceful experience. She can be fully aware of life's troubles and problems and still find a creative way to resolve them. Acknowledging negative and painful feelings does not mean wallowing in them with no hope in sight!

Negativism virtually dominates the world. Many children's magazines have a special "what's wrong with this picture" segment. Even kids' placemats at restaurants have these "what's wrong" pictures. Your daughter is being conditioned from a very early age to be critical and look for the negative, the wrong, the what-doesn't-fit-in, side of life. All this may sound innocent enough, but over time, even young children can learn to be overly critical as their first response.

The positive twist

Life is full of ups and downs. Your daughter will experience her share of painful moments, disappointments, and hurt. She will also see others in horrible situations, struggling with a variety of problems. She need not pretend these things aren't happening. If she can acknowledge them and then choose to respond with confidence and hope, she can help bring others up with her optimism and creative solutions. The world needs her great ideas and energy.

Avoid learned helplessness

Learned helplessness is a term that has been coined to describe people who have literally learned to be and act helpless. They have not developed the confidence nor the skills to solve problems in a positive way. They virtually do not know what to do—what actions or steps to take to resolve problems. They wait around hoping someone will rescue them and fix their problems for them. They have learned to be helpless and hopeless.

Learning to finding positive solutions can be hard work. As you work to teach your daughter to be strong and confident in the face of tough situations she will sometimes feel overwhelmed and uncertain. Encourage her to bring her problems to you for help. As she describes problems, help her break them down into manageably sized pieces. Without blaming, help her identify the cause. Teach her to approach her problems step by step.

Developing a positive attitude

As she struggles with problems, teach her about attitude. Attitude can make or break a situation, turning it from disaster to a great learning experience. It can make people want to help her or turn their backs on her. If she is willing to take responsibility for her part in a conflict, the road to good communication is a lot smoother. No one wants to be blamed. As much as possible, remove the concept of blame from the picture. The "truth," whatever it is, usually gets completely lost anyway. Focus instead on moving forward with good, solid solutions.

Sometimes when your daughter believes she is right, she can get rather prickly. This tends to get the other person's fur up, too. Teach her good listening skills to help diffuse the conflict. Help her to look for something positive and helpful in the situation to help move through the problem. Teach her how to look beyond the conflict or problem to see the larger picture. Refusing to get bogged down in the mess keeps her mind clear to think of answers.

When your daughter starts griping and complaining, help her redirect her thinking to something that will move her forward. Helping her problem-solve gives her a sense of hope and confidence that she can handle and solve her problems. Helping her reframe and put a new attitude and perspective on her viewpoint lifts her out of the doldrums and into a sunnier spot. Her attitude can either drain her vigor or give her a spurt of energy. How she chooses to see situations and respond to them will make or break her own level of happiness. Nobody else, even if they act perfectly, can make her feel happy. Her sense of happiness and well-being has to come from the inside out. As she chooses to identify problems and put a positive twist and a workable solution on them, she can conquer her world.

7

HELPING HER ARTICULATE
HER VALUE

**"We must remember that Ginger Rogers did everything
Fred Astaire did, only backwards and in high heels."**
(Source Unknown)

Your daughter is a rising star striving to reach her zenith. Her future is crackling with possibilities. What can you do to help her capture and articulate her identity so that she can reach her highest potential?

For starters, help her to find her voice. Finding her voice means defining who she is and what she thinks, wants and believes in. Her voice should be strong; she needs the confidence to use it. Developing her self-esteem and finding her voice go hand-in-hand. Soaring requires a solid foundation. She must be rooted deeply in self-confidence and esteem. Help her to be proud of who she is.

It is natural that she will undertake an interior process to explore and define herself; take your daughter's process seriously. No matter what her age, when she sprouts an idea of what or who she wants to be, help her put action on her idea. It doesn't matter that she is going to change her mind a thousand times. Listen to her. Admire her choices and ideas. Let her know she has permission to

119

experiment with her life. She must feel deeply valued to internalize that value into her soul and belief system.

The concept of self-fulfilling prophecy is very real. This is a phenomenon where what your daughter thinks of herself is what she may well become. What your daughter predicts for herself is often eerily correct. That self-prediction arises out of the feedback she receives about herself from the world as well as her own interpretations and perceptions of what she hears and sees. If she is exposed to too much negativity, struggle, and lost and broken dreams she will internalize those messages and believe them to be true. If she is supported and her value honored, she will come to expect good things from life. Her experiences and how she learns to perceive them are the tools that help her create herself.

Not all girls are verbal learners who talk about their feelings or interests. Your daughter may simply show you. She may dance, sing, play baseball, skate, act, or write. Help her add structure and substance to her interests. Kids often need help to learn how to act on their ideas.

Everyone has heard stories of women who, when told they could not do something were egged on to prove they could do something in spite of it all. But why place roadblocks in your daughter's way? Instead, steep her mind and attitudes with messages of confidence and esteem. This does not mean gushing and carrying on every time she wiggles her finger. Nor does it mean falsely building up her hopes with misinformation about her abilities to prevent her feelings from being hurt. When your daughter is struggling and not doing very well, you can reframe the struggle into a positive challenge by breaking it down into manageable bite-sized pieces that will lead to success.

MAKING HEALTHY CHOICES

Moms and dads are encouraged when they realize they can help their daughters weave daily choices and decisions into a legacy of strength. Your daughter can learn to incorporate what she already knows, mix in brand new information, and arrive at a decision that is right for her—one that leaves her feeling proud of herself and on top of the world.

Decision-making patterns

Does your daughter seem to close her eyes and jump into any decision that appeals to her or her peers at any given moment? Does she repeatedly make the same sorry choices that get her in trouble over and over? Or does she freeze, get stuck, and make a no-decision decision? The choices she makes today, large or small, create her tomorrows. Sit down with your daughter before and after she makes a decision. Work with her to see and understand her own pattern of decision making. Don't criticize any odd choices; rather, help her walk through how she arrived at each decision. Look for patterns. These patterns could be thoughts or beliefs she has about how things should be. It could be nothing more than her wanting something bad enough that she just went out and did it. The older your daughter gets the higher the stakes of her immediate gratification decisions.

Getting unstuck

When it's hard for your daughter to make good decisions she may need help to smooth out the process. It's hard for parents, too, when daughters don't make good choices. Parents are left to help pick up the pieces and fix the problem. What are some of the problem areas that girls get stuck on as they try their decision-making wings?

Courage
She may need courage to start making new choices that are different from those of her friends. Girls want to belong; peer pressure can be crushing. She may continue along the same path she's been

on because it feels too hard to be different—the worst possible fate in the minds of many girls. You can't explain away her fears of being different, of making a choice that isn't in sync with her friends' choices, but you can help her walk through the outcome of a variety of choices to take a look at what is in store from each scenario. If she's six, help her look ahead (a difficult cognitive skill at that age) to what might happen—good or bad—if she makes her choice. Will she feel good about herself or will she be in a lot of trouble? If she's eleven, help her figure out what she wants to do aside from what her close-knit group of friends thinks about it. If she's fifteen, help her walk through how her decision will affect her longer-term goals: friendships, college, free-time, money. Every age group (including parents) struggles with slowing down long enough to think through how decisions will affect their future plans. Show your daughter how to stop long enough to make a decision she can honestly feel good about later.

Selfish?

Many girls fear they are being selfish if they assert themselves and do what they want to do. They will avoid conflict at all costs. On the other end of the spectrum is the girl who demands her way most if not all of the time. Girls struggle with feeling that what they say and what they want are not important. They often just keep quiet and go along with the majority, feeling too uncomfortable to speak up. These are symptoms of society's message to girls and women that they should be meek, agreeable, and cooperative, no matter what. How can you know if this is happening with your daughter? Complaining is a big clue. A lot of complaining is just that—griping. But listen closely and see if you find a pattern. Does she complain that one kid in class gets all the recognition? Does one kid get to be the leader, the student council representative, the chosen one year after year? Your daughter may need courage to choose someone else, or to make herself available. Going after the big apple is not selfish, but does your daughter believe that? Moodiness is another clue. When she isn't able to express herself she may become moody and irritable. (See chapter 10 for more). It's definitely more work for her to speak up and state her case but she may be a happier girl as a result.

Stubbornness

This is also known as digging in her heels, refusing to listen to anyone else, plugging her ears, and other charming responses. Stubbornness in and of itself is not a bad trait. In fact, it may be one of her best assets if she learns to use it to her advantage. It's good for her to be stubborn when the going gets rough and she holds to her beliefs. Stubbornness is the push that keeps her going when everybody else wimps out and leaves her standing alone to pursue an important goal. Stubbornness only gets in the way when it prevents her from looking at the whole picture or causes her to suffer. Help her to pry her mind open to accept other possible solutions to her problem. In the spirit of teamwork, present a few ideas she may not have thought of, but don't stuff them down her throat. Encourage her to come up with her own options; let her play around with problems and choices on her own.

Lack of self-trust

Your daughter can use the experiences gained from her decision-making process to increase her ability to trust her own judgment. She may question her own decision-making skills and see herself as weak or not as smart as others. As you talk through her decisions give her credit for her good ideas and creative thinking, even if her idea isn't practical or usable.

Self-value

Teach her to value herself enough to take the necessary steps and actions to achieve the decisions she feels are right for her. Work with her to develop the empowering attitude of "What's right with this picture?" instead of the negative, powerless "What's wrong with this picture?" attitude. Showing her how to take charge of her decisions, playing out the possible scenarios, and problem-solving the roadblocks gives her hands-on experience in solving her own life problems. Don't let her write off her daily life by not paying attention or sluffing off decisions that she has the power to make. How boring to just go along with everyone else's ideas of how life should be. Postponing decisions is postponing life.

AFFIRMING HER GIRLHOOD

Being a girl is a wonderful thing. A girl does not have to be like a boy. She can just be a girl. Affirmations can help your daughter feel good about being a girl. Affirmations are statements that she can make quietly to herself or out loud. They are positive statements that affirm her value and worth as a growing girl. They help to counter the negative messages that she may hear about girls and women in society, in the media, or at school. These statements replace self-doubting thoughts with positive, affirming statements of her girlhood.

It's helpful to design a special "affirmation" for your daughter to counteract any particular area of self-doubt and worry she may have. Homemade affirmations are the best because they are a perfect match for any struggle she may be battling. All you need to do is identify the problem area and then begin selecting words that will help her heal that problem. These words are usually foundation-building phrases that direct her mind to think about the solution rather than the problem. Affirmations are words that offer her hope, comfort, and solutions. They can be written on little cards or pieces of notepaper that she carries with her in her backpack to school. Or tape a few up on her mirror in her room so she sees them every morning before she heads out into her day. She can even keep a little stack of them on her nightstand to read each night before going to sleep and again in the morning. Or, she can tuck them under her pillow. How do you design affirmations? Here are a few general affirmations to give you some ideas and get you started. After you try these out you and your daughter can create your own.

- Being a girl is great! I like being a girl and I like being me. I am _____ (fill in some positive personal characteristics such as strong, smart, happy, good-natured, friendly, and so on).
- I am learning to figure out _____ (name a topic or subject she is struggling with) and am getting better at it everyday!
- I am learning to handle my fear of _____ (whatever). I am bigger and stronger than my fears!
- The more I practice _____ (piano, skating, basketball . . .) the better I am getting!
- I am saving my money for _____ and will soon be able to get it!
- I'm really great at _____ (math, computers, writing, gym).
- I'm safe. It's OK to _____ (go to sleep, go to camp, stay home alone).
- I'm smart and I know I can figure this out!
- My mom and dad love me. So does _____ (my grandma, grandpa, brother, sister, and so on).
- My body looks just great. I like my hair and how I look.

Think up as many as you and your daughter can. Keep them in a special place or have her carry them with her to take out and read periodically throughout the day. Keep a few in her desk at school. The more she can think of, the more she will have these sentences at her command. The more positive input the better.

HERSTORY

"History" is one of those gender-unfriendly words we have become so used to we don't even think about it. Jokes are made and many people roll their eyes as society is introduced to more gender-neutral terms. Although a nationwide effort is being made to change our school texts and job descriptions to become more gender-neutrally balanced, many still devalue the necessity of changing our English language from patriarchal to gender-equal.

We have certainly come a long way to raise our consciousness toward becoming aware of stereotyping and gender bias. Yet a quick game with your daughter may prove how far we have left to go. Name twelve different career titles and ask your daughter if she thinks of a man or a woman for each of the job titles. The results may be startlingly grim. The pink collar ghetto still exists in reality as well as in the minds of young girls planning their futures. Girls still move in chilling masses in the direction of low-pay, low-skill jobs. Their expectations for themselves fall deeply in the hole that even our language has dug for them.

As girls begin their venture through the school system, they will immediately be faced with textbooks filled with men who did things—men who changed the course of history. Where were the women? Where are the women? Parents need to be on top of this issue to instill in growing daughters the validity of the role of women. Parents need to watch their language to make sure it is gender-friendly and doesn't place girls and women in a disadvantageous position.

Language is such a powerful tool. It talks to us about values and influences how we think about life. It describes what we view as important. When people open their mouths they are letting the world in on their thoughts, beliefs, and values. None of us want our daughters surrounded by degrading slang terms for girls and women. Even though she may not be hearing that in your home, she is hearing it on the street, at school, on the bus, and most definitely in the media! Helping your daughter respond to this type of language empowers her to value herself as a girl. Teaching her to think through how to respond to all the different aspects of gender unfriendly language is a big task. How empowered she will be when she is able to point out the gender bias of a school textbook or respond to the gutter language about girls and women she hears on the street or in a movie. She may already be so used to it that she doesn't really hear it! We must teach our girls to hear and respond to this language problem.

When you trace the accomplishments of women past and present as well as heighten awareness of the language we use to describe everyday life you can broaden a girl's perspective on where women fit into the world. Teach your daughter to ascribe power and purpose to the activities of women. This affirms a future that includes her own contributions. Use positive descriptors when you refer to women and you will teach your daughter how you feel about women.

Focus particular attention to what you say about women highlighted positively or negatively in the news, women you encounter during the course of the day, and women and girls who speak out. Common everyday language frequently includes atrocious terms to describe women—how they look, their personal characteristics, their abilities. We see it, we hear it, we usually don't even pay attention anymore. We like to think we have conquered this issue. The schools try to mold language. At home we don't accept certain words. Yet out in the world girls absorb derogatory terminology for women and girls.

Making the shift

Language is an easy way to begin making revolutionary changes in how girls and women are spoken and referred to. Refuse to use derogatory terms. Refuse to pay entertainment dollars to hear girls and women being spoken to in abusive, degrading terms.

Think about job descriptions and use gender-neutral terms. This country has begun much of the work already. Mailmen are mailcarriers, firemen are firefighters, stewardesses are flight attendants, and so on. Where sexism is still rampant is in daily conversation. It's important to stop referring to the female support staff as "the girls at the front desk" or saying things like "schedule your next appointment with my girl." Think about it. When was the last time you heard a group of male doctors or lawyers referred to as the "boy doctors in the next office" or "I have a boy lawyer"? Or made a reference to the "boys at the office"? Any female over the age of eighteen is a woman, not a girl.

Every parents needs to role-model for daughters and sons the need to be watchful of language. Language is subtle, powerful, fluid and everywhere. So is it ever okay to refer to women as girls? When in doubt, don't, but you can ask. Ask a woman if it's okay. Let her decide for herself. Ask your daughter how she feels about it. Notice if she refers to adult women as girls and adult men as men. If so, why? What message is she receiving to make her put grown women in the one-down position of a child, but not men?

Instill pride in your daughter for being a girl growing into a woman. Don't devalue her by referring to her grown-up counterparts as youngsters. If your daughter is young she is still a girl. Teach her to be proud of her girlness. Also teach her that girls grow up to become women.

BANNING FEAR MESSAGES

"Be careful!" we call out to our daughters, our good intentions based in love and concern for them. And yet think about what a deep and disturbing message that is for a daughter to hear. "Be careful." "Maybe you shouldn't do that." "You're going to get hurt." "You'll probably just get yourself all worn out and sick." "You're burning the candle at both ends." "I certainly didn't do that when I was your age." Stricken looks, worried, furrowed eyebrows, powerful body language messages of worry laden with fear—this is parental fear to be exact. On the one hand, it is absolutely appropriate to teach daughters the art of making good decisions and being aware of dangers so that they stay healthy, safe, and happy.

With many parents, however, the line gets crossed to where they unload their own fears onto their daughter. The problem becomes unmanageable when the messages seep in deeper and deeper, year after year. Girls become afraid to try new things, go new places, or stick their necks out. Fear and worry messages are wicked little destroyers of her confidence and her sense of "I can do this!" Girls take these niggling fears with them into adulthood and become women lacking in the confidence that they will be able to make it on their own in this world. The fears and worries expand with each passing year and permeate their consciousness, getting generalized to the rest of life. In rather short order she may become afraid to try new things, uncertain of whether she will be able to take care of herself in various situations. Parents usually don't realize how destructive their own fears are to their daughters because they are adults and believe their advice of caution to be practical, prudent, standard operating procedure. Parents may have become a little too cynical and bitter for their daughters' good. It's true that parents have seen some tough life experiences and would like to prevent their daughters from getting hurt. But it might be a good idea to examine the cautious, fearful, worrisome messages parents may give to their daughters.

Fear is a potent source of control. Not allowing her to venture out on her own restricts her by worry and fear—fear that is not really even her own, fear that, perhaps with loving concern, has been foisted upon her shoulders. Controlling through fear is really not helpful. She has enough to deal with out in the world without dragging along fear and uncertainty. Fear undermines her ability to tackle the problems of life head-on. She may begin to doubt her ability to handle situations; she won't feel up to the task. She may begin to experience feeling sick, fatigued, or shaken when facing a challenge. Worry is an exhausting energy drain. It is a heavy cloud that undermines her natural abilities and joy. She feels less than capable to complete projects or meet deadlines and expectations.

Without throwing healthy caution and practicality to the wind, parents can give their girls appropriate safety measures and common sense. As a parent, you teach her the exhilarating experience of confidence when you allow her to take risks, large and small. Give her the opportunities to try her wings. It's perfectly okay if she falls down and gets banged up. All parents hate to see their daughters hurting—scraped-up emotionally or physically. It's not fun to see a daughter struggling and hanging on a limb of challenge. But if you serve as a guidepost to her as she works it out herself and if you assure her that you will help her figure it out, you send her a

129

tremendously empowering message that she is capable of figuring it out and that she can count on a supportive environment.

We all hate to see a bright girl held back from her full potential by inherited fears. As a parent you can help your daughter sort out her fears and worries and find small, everyday solutions and options to let her move beyond the fear and worry. Does she want to do something that really does make you queasy? Take stock of your concern. Is it real or is it a throwback from your own childhood? Did your parents fill you with fears and concerns? Do your fears really fit this present situation with your own daughter? At times she will want to do something that is not a good plan. Discuss with her the pros and cons of her idea. Help her problem-solve the dilemmas and challenges her choice might present. She is still struggling to learn good judgment and discernment. Guide her thought process without directing her thoughts. Insist that she list the possible negatives of her decision and expect her to come up with at least a few options for how to handle these problems. Letting her blow off reality is not helpful, but neither is popping her balloon. A job of parenting is trying to help your daughter realistically problem-solve without smashing her ideas and dreams with your own backlog of worries. Parents have to strike a balance between alerting their daughters to the realities of the world and instilling in them confidence that they can meet each task and challenge. This is a lot harder on parents than on the girl! At some point parents have to let go and close their eyes as their fresh and energetic daughters take flying leaps of faith that makes parents' hearts quake with mortal terror yet soar with hope and pride.

LISTEN WITH YOUR EYES

Does your daughter have selective hearing, paying attention only when it suits her? Do you feel like just about everything you say goes in one ear and out the other without so much as leaving a trace? It's rather amazing how completely they can filter out what's being said to them. And yet for all our complaining, the truth of the matter is we do the same thing. We feel like our daughters are talking nonstop and we tune out most of what they are saying. My guess is they feel as frustrated and tuned-out as we do. We want our daughters to tell us about their lives and yet we barely take a moment to listen—to really listen. So often, tucked inside of everyday conversations are kernels of truth about our daughter's lives— tidbits of information that we would do well to pay attention to. Smoothly running through the daily trivia is the thread of our daughter's inner life. Whether she is angry and upset, is filling you in on her day, or is barely saying two informative words, try to hear what she is saying about herself and her life. The older she gets, the more silent she will become; getting a complete sentence out of her then may be a goal in and of itself. You will pretty much be left in the cold, to watch, wait, and wonder (and will you ever wonder). What is she thinking, doing, and planning? Where is she going?

Start early to listen with your eyes; it sends a profound message of respect and involvement. Let her see and experience that you are listening to her. Eye contact is a powerful tool that goes a long way toward promoting understanding. It can actually help keep tempers under control because you are listening to more than the words. You are seeing for yourself the body language—the expression in her eyes and on her face. She will also experience the connectedness of being fully heard. Open your eyes! See your daughter for who she really is. Watch her with respect and appreciation as she finds her path through life. Listen closely and carefully with your eyes.

AFFIRMING HER CHOICES

Did your parents or siblings ever talk you out of something you really wanted to do? Did they talk you into doing things their way? Maybe in the long run their idea was better but it was frustrating to settle for what someone else wanted. It is just as frustrating for your daughter when this happens. The world cannot always go her way; it's pleasant for her when she can have some of her smaller wishes met. Try to give her the gift of a positive response to the choices she makes on her own. You don't have to lie blatantly and say you love her choices, but you can find positive, affirming statements to make about them.

Personal choices

It's important to recognize that your daughter's choices, even when they are very different from your own, don't necessarily reflect on you. This is very easy to accept in theory. In reality, it's a lot tougher. We know what we like and often wish our daughters would just magically go along with our preferences. This is usually not the case. She may not want to wear dresses, keep her hair cut short, or read the books you want her to. As she develops a strong personality her own personal choices will begin to show themselves. Try to take an honest look at yourself and decide how much you need to influence her choices (for example, yes, she needs boots in the middle of a Midwestern winter, like it or not) and where you can begin letting go and giving her more freedom.

Mismatched Socks?

Every parent has different expectations about how her or his daughter should look. Some parents let their daughter pick out any outfit she wants. They are willing to sacrifice "good taste" for creativity. These parents have creative girls who often like to wear mismatched socks. Then there are parents who feel it's their duty to instill in their daughter some sense of what "goes together" in hopes that her choices will reflect this more refined approach. Some parents care if their daughter buttons up her jacket when it's snowing outside, others believe their daughter can make up her own mind. Whatever your parenting style, it's okay. The real issue at hand is allowing her to own her choices and freedom within the structure and family rules you set. Try to be consistent; don't give her double messages. Don't tell her, "It's your choice honey, but I sure would-n't wear that outfit if I were you." She's going to feel obligated to go with your choice because she was made to feel uncomfortable with any other.

On the other hand, you can let her know that it's okay that the two of you may have different preferences and will make different choices. If you have a set idea in mind and want specific behavior from her, be clear about it. Tell her she can choose whichever dress she would like, but she does have to wear a dress to the wedding reception. Don't double-bind her by telling her a choice of clothing is completely up to her, then staying mad at her all afternoon for choosing the "wrong" outfit. Telling her, in essence, that she "looks stupid in that outfit" isn't helpful to her self-esteem. If you smile and tell her she looks like she just stepped out of a magazine ad (which is probably completely true given today's clothes for kids) it will leave her feeling great.

Then there is the hair issue, which is always a riot (sometimes almost literally). To this day I wear my hair long because I always got talked into cutting it really short as a kid. I hated it. It's thick and dry and when it's short, it sticks out like Moses and the burning bush. Then my ugly little "pixie" haircut (remember those?) would get worse from curling up the tiny, little wet ends in bobby pins. In the morning I looked like a freak! I don't care what anybody said, I did not look one bit "cute!"

Because anything goes in the hair department these days, your daughter will have quite a selection to choose from. She might want to try something new or something similar to her best friend's hair-do. Maybe you have a daughter who absolutely could not care less about her hair. Decide whether you intend to be part of the haircut process. Can she do whatever she wants or not? Is the sky the limit or do you get to put the lid on it? Once you give her carte blanche you will have to stick to it whether you like her new style or not. Telling her you don't like her haircut is unkind. Telling her you're glad she got such a fun haircut for herself is affirming. If she's miserable with her new do, assure her it will grow out; give her some

133

idea how long it will take. When you let her make her own decision you keep her from complaining endlessly about hating her hair.
If she begged for months to get a perm and even had to contribute
some of her own money for it (!) she will be a lot less inclined to
whine about it if she hates it. She will simply suffer in silence (at
least she will be quiet around you!) Hair and clothes are not that
important. Your daughter is more than a head of hair or a trendy
new outfit. Remember the saying, "Don't sweat the small stuff." Hair
and clothes are just a small form of personal expression.

A space of her own

A room of her own. What a wonderful thing to have. At any time in
our lives, how delicious it is to have a room to call our own. All
ours. To do with, decorate, hide out in, relax in, work in as we
please. When you walk into your daughter's room where every
square inch of wall space is covered with decorations and her ceiling is a veritable Michelangelo of hanging designs and her desk
looks like it blew up, control your temper and frustration. Even
though her room looks like a disaster tell her that you realize she is
actually a very creative girl who has great design ideas. Could she
simply humor you and pick up the stuff that is not part of the over-
all Master Design Plan? (I found this one works very well. Despite
my efforts to control the chaos, my youngest's room is a disaster,
but admittedly, she is incredibly creative. She informs me, "I'm creative, Mom. Creative people don't clean up.") We even have a criteria for a clean room that surpasses all possible threats. It's joking-
ly referred to as "Mother-clean." When the room is Mother-clean, it
meets the highest standards of picked-up-ness (without interfering
with her creative genius). Mother is happy. Let the company come.

Set up your bottom-line expectations. Insisting that she follow
some family code of cleanliness is a good opportunity for her to
learn to care about her environment. You can teach your daughter
to care about her room and your home. You are not doing her any
favors if you let her roam the house or apartment with no personal
responsibility. Assign her homekeeping tasks. Inform her the maid

is not working today and so it's up to her to help keep the family home in a livable state. Such is life. It is not your job as a parent to run around after her like a personal attendant. Let her make her personal choices about how she wants to keep and decorate her room within the basic guidelines you set. She will begin to value her homespace as her parents teach her to do so. Kids tend to value what parents value. Teach her in your own way how to take care of her things and to respect the space called home. Mansion or efficiency apartment, it's your home, it's her home. Make it homey.

Hand-picked relationships

One of the biggest and yet most fluid choice points your daughter will make continually throughout her life is her relationships. Parents feel great when their daughters hang around with polite, happy, healthy, and intelligent kids. Parents are elated when daughters choose respectful, educated, hardworking boys with just the smallest touch of rebel to make them interesting. What's not so happy a scene is when parents don't approve of a daughter's choice of girl- or boyfriends. Are parents supposed to grit their teeth and smile or do they get to say something? It's a decidedly touchy subject with countless opinions. If your daughter is going to get hurt or become involved in areas you absolutely do not want her caught up in, you may have to step in. Depending on her age, you will have more or less influence. When you can, focus on supporting and affirming her good choices in relationships. Talk with her, but more important, show her how you work hard to choose good, healthy relationships for yourself and what you do to nurture them and keep them going. Realize what a powerful role model you are in the relationships department. Do you choose friends, male or female, that build you up and make you a better person? Or do you choose friends, male or female, that aren't good or healthy for you, that treat you poorly or take advantage of you? Share with her how you choose to handle relationships without bashing anyone in the process.

Give her room to mull over her relationships and try not to

judge or be critical. You don't, however, have to be a perfectly restrained parent. If you see her heading down the path of a destructive relationship, say so. Express your concerns. If she will let you in, help her problem-solve the relationship conflicts. If she's in first grade and always teams up with the kid in the class who throws things across the room, you have more power and influence. If she's a teen and you're dealing with the boyfriend from hell, don't push her; rather challenge her with the reality of how she is being treated. Whether she is young or a teen talk to her about her friend's behavior and how it affects others. Relationships are mirrors back to her, showing her part of her own self. Relationships with friends will bring out her best qualities and biggest areas of struggle. She will see a part of herself in the faces and behaviors of her friends. Use the friendships she forms to let her learn about herself. Support her as much as you can to make her own friendship choices.

Time to choose

Your daughter has opportunities each week to make choices about how to spend her time. She can learn to choose wisely. She will need added coaching with this issue; the concept of time is abstract to her. Give her options to choose from rather than wide-open, endless choices; it will help her hone her decision-making skills. As she makes choices about after-school activities, groups to join, classes to take, camps to attend, and lessons to take, affirm her decisions. Support her choices while helping her understand the commitment involved with each. Be sure you also feel prepared to play whatever role you need to play (for example, chauffeur, coach, volunteer, and so on) before she officially signs away her time. This is a good time to practice negotiating skills. Don't just threaten, "Now remember, I am not going to stay late and clean up after you." Instead, clearly indicate exactly what you are willing to do. That way you are working as a team and you can wholeheartedly support her decisions. If her decision doesn't obligate you in any way, try to let go, allow her to make her own choice, and learn how it feels to live with it. Doing this now is great practice for bigger, more permanent choices she will need to make later on. When you allow her the joys of personal choice, you affirm her ability to make good decisions for herself; you tell her she is an individual and not a clone. She doesn't have to design her space, her time, or her looks around anyone but herself.

TRACING HER FOOTSTEPS

You know when your parents sometimes give you something they found in the attic that you made back in grade school? The slow smile that spreads across your face, accompanied by rolling eyes, laughter, and an unleashed flood of memories? It's fun to see yourself little again, to remember, to retrace your steps. Sometimes you remember wishing the ground would have opened up that year and swallowed you whole. Sometimes you wish that creepy little brother of yours who tortured you all year would have fallen off the face of the earth. Sometimes you remember your grandma and how funny her laugh was and how she always brought you neat stuff. Sometimes you remember your teacher and how you thought she was the most beautiful lady (or the meanest) you had ever known. Good or bad, the memories are priceless (except, of course, memories of abuse). Our memories are a gift. All of us love to be remembered and hear the stories of our lives.

Memory journals

This idea can be molded into as small or large a project as you would like it to be. You don't have to be a great writer; your daughter truly won't care. The idea is to write down her life as she is living it. Buy a special three-ring notebook that you keep in a very specific, you-can-always-find-it kind of place. You can begin anytime. It doesn't matter whether she is three or fifteen. You can write daily, weekly, monthly, or annually at a special occasion such as a significant holiday, her birthday, or Mother's or Father's Day. Write about your daughter: her life, something she did, something funny, something poignant. Write down the events, the moments, the tiny pieces you wish to never forget. Write the funny or outrageous things she says, the struggle she overcame, her personality traits. Record her friends, family events, projects she completed, ideas she espoused. Remind her of what was important to her then, let her see snippets of her life through your eyes. And don't forget to tell her how you felt about her during these moments. Remind her of how furious you were when she cut off all her hair and that of her friend playing barber shop, pounded nails in the wall to hang her paper pictures, stayed out all night without calling. Fill her in on how proud-to-bursting you were when she accomplished something so important it surprised you all, including her. Remind her of the morning she unexpectedly brought you breakfast in bed, won the trophy, or traveled abroad. Take a moment to tell her how much you have always loved her—no matter what—and how much you always will. Put words on her life. Put shape on her memories. Give her something to get her hands and thoughts around in years to come. Don't leave anything out. It's all a part of her life. Nothing has to be hidden, just treated with respect, dignity, and humor.

Place these treasured memories in the notebook. It doesn't matter whether it's a once-a-year entry or whether it ends up being 2000 pages over time. When she is nearing her eighteenth birthday, take the notebook to a bookbinder, who for a small fee will bind the pages as a hardcover book. They can also make a copy for you. The binder can emboss a title in gold on the cover. Present this lifelong treasure to her at her birthday or graduation. It is a labor of love, the gift of memory to ensure that she will never forget her story.

DEVELOPING FINANCIAL INDEPENDENCE

Responsible parenting includes teaching girls to be financially responsible. It does not matter whether your family lives simply, sticks to a modest budget, or has money to burn. Your daughter must learn to be in control of her finances. If she does not learn early, she will not know how to be in charge of her money when she must depend on her ability to support herself. Face it, everything costs money in this world. In this society people are punished for not having money or for making financial mistakes. The lessons in this chapter are not to devalue the importance of intangibles such as love, health, friendships, and the like. It simply focuses on the imperative that your daughter understand basic finance firsthand.

Do you hand your daughter money for everything? Or do you always have to say "no" to what she wants because you do not have enough money yourself? Does she know how to save for something special, or does everything just appear in the form of freebies and gifts? Does money even mean anything to her? Does your daughter know what it means to "earn" real income? Too many parents think, "Oh, let her be a kid. She'll have to face all those worries soon enough." Unfortunately, this can be a classic setup for her to fail. I always have to shake my head when I hear older students assert that they have to pay for everything themselves. Yet, when asked where the money comes from that they use to pay for everything, the answer is invariably "My parents." They still don't quite see the point; sadly, neither do most of the parents.

When my oldest daughter was eight years old, her school class was going on a camping trip requiring a rather substantial tuition. This was a perfect opportunity for her to earn some of the money herself. I was saddened to learn that out of an entire class of kids my daughter did not know of any other kid who had to earn a portion of the money! All of the other parents, probably without thinking, simply handed their daughters checks. What a lost opportunity to teach her how to scout out jobs, work for income, and receive the message loud and clear that no one is going to hand her money just because she needs it. (For money-earning ideas for girls too young to work out of the home, see "Earning Money at Home," pages 153-57.)

Financial ownership is vital to your daughter's well-being. Many people disclaim the value of having a lot of money. Let your daughter decide for herself what a lot of money is. Let her decide which opportunities she wants to purchase in this lifetime and then help her set in place a foundation that will allow her to achieve her goal. The belief that money is not important needs to be a personal one; it is not one that you should foist on your daughter without letting her have an opportunity to decide for herself. Teaching her financial responsibility and power is not teaching her greed! She must have money to have a place to call home, a car, and the ability to travel and pursue her hobbies and interests. She must have money to support herself and any family she may have later on. She cannot expect anyone else to pay her way in this life. She may choose to share financial responsibility with others but should never become dependent on someone else to support her.

Most parents realize the consequences of too little money and do not want their daughters to have to suffer this fate. Parents do not want their daughters to have to "nickel and dime it" through life. If your daughter does not keep track of her money or earn enough she will walk down the path of bounced checks, poor credit, and threats from creditors. She could ultimately end up bankrupt. It is unfortunate that this society still punishes people for not having money. The very people who struggle daily and can least afford service charges get penalized for not having the right amount of money by the due date on bills. Girls need to know how to avoid these common problems with concrete, specific methods. General messages about "paying your bills on time" are not enough. They need to learn how to not fall behind, but to stay on top and even get ahead!

THE REAL WORLD OF
FINANCIAL RESPONSIBILITY

Most girls grow up in families that need to adhere to a realistic financial budget. This provides an opportunity for them to learn creative ways to gather money. It is hard for any girl to learn financial responsibility if every single thing is just handed to her year after year after year. She could easily grow up being financially dependent.

When you teach your daughter financial responsibility, you give her a lifelong gift that she can tinker with until it suits her personality and choice of lifestyle. It's never too early to begin showing her the reality of money. It is never appropriate or helpful, however, to frighten her or in any way make her feel responsible for the family's finances.

Heightening her awareness about money can be done casually and easily in daily and weekly activities. Rather than grumbling at her for not finishing her plate of food and mumbling about the cost of groceries, suggest she come along to the grocery store. Let her punch the cost of each item into a pocket calculator. Chances are, her eyes will pop as you travel down the aisles. In fact, you may have to reassure her that you were already planning to spend that much money and that you do have enough. Kids are flabbergasted to realize how much money their parents spend at the grocery store. As your daughter gets older, you can begin to expand on this grocery store lesson by having her divide the grocery bill by a typical hourly wage. Help her figure out how many hours of work are needed to eat for a week. It's a prime opportunity to have her play around with career options to learn how easy or hard it is to buy groceries with different career choices.

Handing your daughter money for every financial encounter in her life is sending her an erroneous and dangerous message that someone will always pay her way, that she will never have to think about it. In reality, nothing could be further from the truth. Of course parents have the responsibility to meet most of the financial needs of young girls and the rest of the family. The point is to raise her consciousness and teach her to take control of her daily and future financial circumstances. As she acquaints herself with the reality of purchasing power, she will be processing vital information to help her make career choices. The more time she has to experiment when the stakes are small, the better chance she will have of making healthy and thoughtful choices for herself, ones that she can live with—happily.

ECONOMIC INDEPENDENCE
HER OWN CHECKING ACCOUNT

Did you know that as soon as your daughter is able to sign her name in cursive she can open a checking account? Pretty neat, huh? Why would you want to help her do this at age seven? Because that is not too early to teach her how to keep track of her money— month by month, year by year. Unfortunately, sometimes even large banks don't really think in those terms. When I brought my oldest daughter to one of the largest banks in the city and told the banker I wanted to open a checking account for my seven-year-old, she looked at me blankly and asked, "Why?" I explained that I wanted my daughter to be able to keep track of her money and know at the end of the year where it all went. Even bankers need educating!

Your daughter will burst with pride to have her own checking account. She will be happy to prove to her friends she really has a checking account, proudly whipping out her checkbook to show them.

Owning a checking account at a very early age can be the beginning of your daughter's learning how to track her money. Depending on her age, you may also want to add your own name to the account; not all places of business will honor a check that is only in a minor's name. Also, you will want to go to the county offices to obtain a picture ID card for proper check-writing and cashing identification.

Each month is another opportunity to sit down with your daughter and help her balance her checkbook. Even if no checks were written or deposits made, she will have a chance to read a bank statement. By the time she has her first job, she will be a pro at balancing her monthly financial statements!

Give her a modicum of control over her money, hold her responsible for balances and good record-keeping; this will teach her basic skills as well as impart the message that she is responsible for her own money. If you teach her how to handle money now you will save her a lot of grief in the future.

ECONOMIC INDEPENDENCE

HER OWN SAVINGS ACCOUNT

A personal savings account is a chance for your daughter to watch her money grow into a chubby little nest egg that she can use for something of great importance (or it can simply be a permanent financial backup for her). Many parents have a savings account for college fund for their daughters. This is wonderful. However, I suggest she own her own account that she contributes to herself. She could take a portion of her allowance, gift checks, or money earned. Even quarters add up!

Teach her how to complete deposit and withdrawal slips. Each month take a few minutes to help her read her bank statement and track her progress. If she's five, keep it simple. As she grows older, add more information. Show her how to call the bank after hours and complete transactions over the phone. Help her understand the concept of interest. Speaking of interest, have you ever borrowed a couple of dollars from her allowance jar to pay for the pizza delivery? Be sure you tell her. Add interest when you repay her. Explain how it all works and model responsible behavior.

It's also fun to help her dream about how she would like to use the money. What magical amount would she enjoy watching become a reality through her own achievements? Use this account to help her figure out how much $100, $1000, and even $10,000 really are. It's a great opportunity to help her expand her horizons financially and start to grapple with the larger financial world.

Teach her how to stretch her mind around money—to learn to control her money and not have her money control her. Help her ponder what kinds of "emergencies" might come up that she would deem acceptable to dip into her nest egg. If she is only twelve and an "emergency" is a new fad item she wants to buy, this is your chance to help her make wise choices about her money. Incidentally, this does not mean you talk her out of her purchase. It means you carefully watch her experience her own learning process. Perhaps you have put an absolute limit on the amount she must maintain in her savings, but beyond that it's a great chance for her to learn about making disappointing and sometimes foolish financial choices at an early age when the stakes are small and she can rebuild her nest egg. If she chooses to purchase something useless and flimsy and it breaks on the way home, your heart breaks for her, but what a powerful lesson she has learned.

THREE JARS TO SUCCESS
A CREATIVE APPROACH TO ALLOWANCE

Do you ever wonder about allowances? When to start? How much? Should it be tied to work? Talking to your friends might give you some ideas as well as food for thought about how other families handle the big A.

One idea is to present your daughter with three special jars. These could be intriguing antique jars you have scrounged up at an antique show, or just plain old peanut butter jars. Or let your daughter choose something she likes. All she really needs is a container with a secure cover. Often it is more fun if the container is see-through; that way she can watch her money grow.

Jar #1 is for spending

Every family has to decide for themselves how much this amount should be. This is money she can have strictly for herself. It's a great chance for her to try money on for size. Let her make her own decisions and live with the consequences. If she begs you at the store to purchase something with an "I promise to pay you back from my allowance jar as soon as I get home," hold her to it! Don't forget to collect the money from her. Hold her accountable for her financial decisions. It is unfortunate if it falls apart halfway home, but again, a valuable lesson is learned. Because it involves her own money, it won't take her long at all to put two and two together and start making more sound decisions. This jar should be for her own decision-making skills. It should not be used for punishment. Don't withdraw money she has already accumulated from her jar if she does something rotten. Also, don't withhold allowance.

Think about it. What if you worked hard at your job all week, then your boss withheld your paycheck because of something you messed up on. If you're on commission, you would not earn anything, but that's different. Besides, daughters aren't on commission.

Jar #2 is for sharing

Have her place a certain percentage of the money she receives into her sharing jar. This jar presents an opportunity to broaden your daughter's perspective on the world. It is an opportunity to teach her compassion—her obligation to consider and act on behalf of others less fortunate than herself. This will put some muscle and action on that tired "those less fortunate" statement. She can consider donating to causes that are near and dear to her heart and offer them financial support. As you go through the year, point out to her articles or news reports that she might be interested in. If she is able, have her begin to make a list. At the end of the year support her in choosing one or more of the people, organizations, or causes that seem important to her. Help her sit down and write a letter and enclose a check (from her own checking account, of course) to the place of need she has chosen. If she tells them a little about herself and why she chose them, she may receive a personal letter of thanks. She can then add this to her memorabilia box (see chapter 12).

Jar #3 is for savings

This percentage goes into her personal savings account at the bank. You may wish to set an amount that must always remain in savings and cannot be withdrawn. It is encouraging to watch the jar fill up and then be taken to the bank. Show her how to fill out her own deposit slips; have a special place to keep the slips for balancing with her monthly bank statement. Incidentally, make sure your bank knows it is an account for a minor so that they do not assess a monthly service fee.

TALK MONEY!

It has never been considered very dainty to talk about money, but if your daughter doesn't learn to say the "M" word, loud, clear, and strong, how will she ever feel comfortable handling it, earning it, spending it, or asking for it?

Many girls and women tend to be shy and hesitant about asking for the money that is due them. Many also go to great pains to disclaim that they completed a project for the sheer purpose of making money. It is as if wanting to get money for something they did were a despicable and embarrassing flaw. Parents are often concerned that they are going to turn their daughters into greedy, dreadful, material girls. To avoid this outcome they continue the conspiracy of silence about the "M" word. Let's let the cat out of the bag. The secret is out! Money is healthy. It is just a form of energy that is given back to your daughter in exchange for energy she has put out. The key concept is energy she put out. Give her the message from the beginning that money is returned to her as she is willing to use her talents and abilities. Let her know loud and clear that she can't sit around and hope that someone will rescue and support her! Have discussions with her now about her ideas concerning money and men. How much if any does she think a man is supposed to support her? What is her role in supporting herself and her family?

Does she think and dream small? That's okay, but is it because she is afraid or unsure of how to earn money? Does she know how to turn what she is interested in into cold, hard cash? Do the words cold, hard cash give you the chills? Are you frowning as you read this, conjuring up visions of a money-grubbing female? Parents need to come to grips with their own issues about money or more often than not, lack of money. Resolve your own fears and frustrations about this powerful, fascinating form of energy. Why is it so hard for some people to scrape together a minimum living while with others whatever they touch seems to turn to gold?

An important lesson for your daughter is the correlation between her decisions and the amount of money she brings in. It may be completely appropriate to bring in a smaller amount. But is this at the expense of her dreams? Is it because she can't figure out

147

alternatives and options? Is she missing out on the doors and windows of opportunity? Living simply is vastly differently than living with a simplistic, poverty mentality. Does she believe she will always just scrape by, barely having enough, always having to scrimp for any little luxury? Or does she just assume that someone is always going to be there to provide her with money to spend? Where do you as parents fit into her plans about future money? In her mind, are you going to continue to be her chief source of income? Where does she get this belief? Does she have an inflated, unrealistic vision of having tons of money but no real plan of exactly how she is going to create this money in her life?

Money and personality

Help her figure out how much energy she wants to put into earning money. Is she a young woman who throws herself into a project and works night and day to finish it? Or is she an easygoing girl who takes life a little slower and more methodically? What is her personal style and how can she incorporate it into designing the type of lifestyle she wants to create? Does she count and recount her allowance, calculating the grand total or is she completely clueless about how much she has and couldn't care less anyway?

For your daughter to figure this all out, she will need to learn to talk money. She will need to learn to be specific and speak in a clear voice when discussing how much she will be earning. How much money means to her will figure into her decisions. Yet, as moms and dads you should teach her that her services have value. Teach her how to negotiate her babysitting or lawn care jobs. Unfortunately, many a girl who babysits or mows lawns looks sheepish and claims "Oh, it doesn't matter . . . whatever you want to pay me is okay. . . ." and her voice dwindles and fades as she shrugs her shoulders and looks down at the floor! How on earth is she ever going to know, as an adult woman, how to negotiate a starting salary, contract, or raise if she isn't taught? And who is going to teach her, if not you? Do you know how to ask for a raise or

148

negotiate a fee for your services rendered? If not, take a class and read books ASAP. Your daughter needs a clear, confident, and strong role model. She doesn't need a millionaire, but she does need an adult who knows and believes in her or his own worth and is able to parlay talents into income.

Money-talk ideas

Wages
Show her exactly how to decide on how much to charge for her services, and how to negotiate with her "employer" whether it's you, a neighbor, a friend, or a "referral."

Money discussions
Have casual and formal conversations about the value of money: What is it? How do we use it? Is it important?

Attitudes about money
Examine your own attitudes about money. Specifically, what are your attitudes about girls and money and women and money? Do you tell yourself it's not really important? Do not try to equate it with intangibles such as health, love, well-being. That would be like comparing apples and oranges. It's great to have your health and it's OK to have money. What messages are you powerfully passing on to your daughter about money? Is she learning that if only your family had more money, more stuff, then you would all be happier? Or is she oblivious to where all the money comes from and how it gets into the household?

Independent money decisions
Support your daughter to make her own decisions about money. Money or a lack of money is such a powerful force in the world that it's hard for most parents not to impose their beliefs, values, and philosophies about money onto their daughters.

Try to sort out honestly your beliefs about money. Talk openly and honestly with your daughter about this powerful form of energy that allows her an array of choices to move freely about this world. Money buys choices, options, free time, basic needs, health insurance, and experiences. Responsible financial management can lead to your daughter's peace of mind.

Teach her to plan and make decisions that open doors for her. Show her how to talk about money easily and confidently. Impart to her how she is responsible for herself. Your financial security or lack of financial security should not become the foundation for her future. She must learn money firsthand, for herself.

THE MARKETPLACE

It can be a real kick for your daughter to watch her real or imagined nest egg grow. Play the stock broker game with your daughter. Spend some time exploring the business section of your newspaper. Talk with your own investment advisor or someone you know who likes to work the stock market. Maybe even purchase a book on understanding the market. Pick out a few magazines with financial information and tips. Then go to work on working and playing the stock market. For real or fantasy. The goal? To provide your daughter with a firsthand working knowledge of how the stock market works. You don't have to be a market veteran yourself. You can be as naive and new to the market as your daughter. Just go ahead and have some fun!

Scrounging up the money

The first order of business is to decide whether this is going to be for real or a fantasy investment. If you are a seasoned investor, you may want to provide your daughter with a small amount that she can play with and have authority over. You must then be willing to pay the broker fees and eat the loss, if there is one, without criticizing your new-to-the-market daughter. Decide ahead of time exactly how much she will be allowed to control and whether you have any other stipulations about buying or selling her stocks and bonds.

If this is a fantasy investment, it's still vitally important to prepare yourselves thoroughly. Decide exactly how much money you are going to invest and how much of a loss you are willing to withstand before you sell your stock and try something else. Have your simulation be as realistic as possible for your daughter to begin to get an accurate picture of how the market works. Decide how much you can contribute over the next six months to your portfolio so you are truly budgeting accurately. Because it's a fantasy simulation you are free to invest thousands, even millions of dollars if you so choose. The point is to make sure you stay within your previously assigned budget.

You and your daughter can even start a savings jar to put toward real, future investments. Decide if you want to start small, say $100 or so, and work and save her money until she has enough to invest. Remember, real brokers require real commissions, so add that into your savings plans.

Picking your stock

Sit down with your daughter every week and devour the business and stocks and bonds sections of the paper for a few weeks. Spread them out on the kitchen table and explore them together. Get a handy, paperback reference guidebook that provides definitions for all the hieroglyphics you will encounter. Compare what you see happening in the daily papers with the articles you read in a few investment magazines that you picked up at the bookstore. Is there a company that you think is going to show strong potential growth? Are you reading hot news about a new product being debuted at ABC company? Would you like to try your hand at investing? If so:

Plot strategy

Stocks, the Bond market, Mutual Funds, IRA accounts? Blue-chip stocks or high risk, speculative investments for a potential windfall? A high-yield mutual fund? Whatever you and your daughter decide on, it's a great time to explore personality styles as part of her learning about how money fits into her life and how she responds to it. Help her become acquainted with what kind of an investor she is: risky and foolhardy? conservative and buttoned-down? Remember she has to work with the budget she has designated—no borrowing. If she bombs, she's out the "money." If she has a fabulous return on the dollar, what will she do with her money? Reinvest? Travel? All this is information to her about who she is in relation to money.

Tracking

She should watch, track, and record her own progress. Don't let her make real or fantasy investments and then just let them ride off into the sunset without her. Keep discussing strategy. Support her learning process. Make keeping track fun and educational so that she begins to grasp how her decisions affect her investments. If you have a personal computer, track her stock portfolio on spreadsheets. If not, handwrite her progress. However she chooses to keep track of her portfolio is fine, just stick to it.

Financial role models

If you have a financial advisor or broker, bring your daughter along to meet her or him. Introduce her to the world of professional financial advisors: people who can help her understand the market and guide her in her decision making. If you don't have an advisor or broker, ask around. Someone is bound to know someone who is acquainted with the stock market and would be willing to spend a little bit of time mentoring your daughter in the world of stocks and bonds. It's important for her to talk one-to-one with someone knowledgeable even if she doesn't have the resources right now to invest actual cash. If possible, she should meet women who work in the world of finance: women out in the professional world who handle large sums of cash for profit; women who make their living in the world of money.

Worldwide markets

Broaden your daughter's view of the financial world by introducing her to the other stocks and bonds markets worldwide. Read and learn about the Japanese market. How does trading on it (while we sleep here in the USA) affect the US market?

Introduce her to other forms of investments as well. You don't have to know anything about them yourself. This can be a fun learning process for you, too, as your family explores the world of high finance. Read articles in newspapers and magazines that introduce her to collectibles for investment purposes, the world of gold and silver trading, and auction houses filled with priceless artifacts to be sold to the highest bidder. If she's old enough, tune in to "Wall Street Week" and listen to the financial discussions. If she's young, keep it simple and interesting. If you are ever in New York, visit Wall Street and the New York Stock Exchange. Let her see the monies of the world being wildly traded and transformed into fortunes or ruin. Money is a fluid, flowing form of energy. Introduce her to the place where money and fortunes rise and fall every day. Money can be great fun. It doesn't have to always be a serious, scary, worrisome thing. Let her play with it. Let her invest in her future by learning the ropes now.

EARNING MONEY AT HOME

If your daughter is too young to hold a "real" job or if for any other reason she doesn't have a job yet, a good place to start is to put her to work at home! This is an important place to start whatever her age. Without dumping all the crummy tasks on her, it's surprising how much your daughter could help lighten your own work load by helping out with chores around the homefront. This will help her work on learning how to plot strategy for earning money, be responsible for starting and completing assigned tasks and being part of the home work-team.

To pay or not to pay?

Being a part of a family includes basic responsibilities that simply have to be done and don't warrant a "paycheck." Everyone in the family has to participate in keeping things running somewhat smoothly; the payback is some sense of order and comfort. Somebody has to cook and that somebody probably won't get paid for it. Grocery-shopping and errand-running aren't very lucrative, either. These same kinds of thankless tasks exist for your daughter. Each family has to decide for themselves which tasks are money-earners and which ones are just plain old chores that need to be done by everyone living in your home. Some common freebies might include having your daughter be responsible for feeding the pooch or the cat, clearing the dinner table every night (I cook, they clean-up), clean up after herself when she's done in the bathroom whether it's a shared bathroom or her own, emptying her full-to-overflowing wastebasket once a week, making her bed in the morning, shutting the door behind her when she goes in or out, and putting away anything she decides to take out and use. If she uses the scissors and tape, it's not your job to put it away for her, nor is that a money-making task.

Basic common sense and courtesy tasks are part of learning to live together in harmony and order. If the kitchen or family room constantly looks like a pig-sty maybe it's time to sit down together as a family and draw up a plan to keep things at least this side of chaos. It's not just the parents' responsibility to keep the lid on disaster. Your daughter can learn important group living skills and basic personal responsibility without getting paid for it. It's a valuable lesson when she learns pride in contributing toward making her home as livable and comfortable as possible.

Working for pay

On the other hand, separating out a few of the larger home tasks and turning them into opportunities to earn money teaches her to take on larger projects and get rewarded for her hard work. This also teaches her about commitment. Help her figure out which projects she has the time and energy to not only start, but finish. Working on home projects for pay is separate from her regular allowance. The philosophy and intent behind working at home for pay is different from that of an allowance. Working for pay, she is taking on a project that would otherwise have to be done by someone else. It's not those daily tasks that are simply her own personal responsibility to complete. These are not tasks such as cleaning up after herself. These are jobs you are willing her pay her to do. Perhaps each week she can do one to three small jobs for money. As she takes on these jobs she can begin to keep track of her earned money. She can plan to save up for an item she would like or attach her own reward.

Job jars

Some families have a job jar. This is a large jar filled with all the tasks that need to be done around the house. They can include big projects such as painting the garage or projects that keep repeatedly showing up, such as mowing the lawn or running back and forth with the laundry in an apartment. Each piece of paper can list the task and the amount being paid for it. By clearly stating at the beginning how much it's worth, you save a lot of time and energy haggling over price. Anyone can put anything in the job jar. She can even give away some of her own work to any other takers as long as she is willing to pay to have it done. From time to time my youngest (a born-messy kid) pays her older sister (an orderly pack-rat) to clean off her bookshelves which have become a disaster beyond belief. They strike a deal and everyone is happy. One loves to clean and one would sooner eat a bug than pick anything up. One gets paid to do what she loves to do and the other one just has to make sure to keep an eye on her finances so she can pay to get rid of her onerous tasks. What a deal!

Moms and dads do not have to do every project around the house. As your daughter gets older she will be able to take on many of these one-time and routine projects. Paying her for them helps her learn to plan her time and get paid for time and energy spent. You are helping her to make the work/living connection. Not having to work for anything sends a lethal message to her that everything is just going to magically get done and she doesn't have to be responsible for any of it.

Team projects

Your family can also decide to take on a team project. The "pay" includes the fun of working together, getting silly, and finishing the project off with a group reward such as ordering pizza or going to the movies or the mall. Here she is learning to be part of a working group that knows how to have fun. Paint the garage, dig a bigger garden, wash the windows, do a serious clean and wax on the family car(s). Pick a weekend and go to work. You could polish off more than one major project if you all work together. If she's four years old she will need a lot of loose time to ding around. But do hold her to being a part of the group. Don't let her completely wander off and detach from the group. Keep her involved. Let her be the "leaf patrol" picking up all the stray leaves as you rake, or chief-in-charge of keeping the tools in one spot, or being the "go-fer" for whatever is needed. She will feel important and be a true contributor. If she's fifteen, she's old enough to stick around and help finish. She can't fly off just because her friends call and want to run off after lunch. Help her feel a part of the team and the finished product. Cleaning the gutters is a drag but when it's done even she can feel some sense of accomplishment!

However your family decides to work out the chores, follow through with your plans. Stick to it so she knows she has a source of potential income available to her in exchange for her time and energy. Besides, when you allow her to take on some of the home responsibilities, you buy yourself some free time!

MAD MONEY

Every family deserves a mad money jar—a special jar stuffed with stray coins and occasional dollar bills that add up to fun. We have a small wooden bank made out of an antique post office box, replete with glass door and combination lock. It sits on the piano and every time somebody has some loose change to put away, they drop it in the post office box bank. Whatever you choose to use, welcome everyone to drop in a few coins periodically. It takes a while but all those coins and dollar bills do add up and every few months, there's just enough money to purchase some small treat. We use ours for entertainment only. Tickets, ice cream cones, lunch out, pizza, whatever. There is usually only enough to do some small- to moderate-priced activity. Half the fun is dumping out the coins, adding up the "millions" and deciding how to spend the fortune. It's a good educational experience for the young ones, too!

It's such a small thing, but it is one more opportunity to include your daughter in accumulating her available fortunes. You can involve her in financial decisions in a myriad of ways. This one has no big expectations and is intended only for fun and frolic. This is one case where she can be part of a group—everyone contributes, everyone gets a say in spending it, everyone gets to enjoy it. Let her experience the lighter side of money. After all, how often (for anyone) does money get to be viewed with such casual abandon—easy come, easy go? Everyone needs a little mad money!

THE CORNUCOPIA OF COMPOUNDING

Do you want to hear some really wild numbers? You'd better sit down for this one! Following is a table of incredible numbers if you save $25, $50, or $100 a month for your daughter. As a parent, saving for your daughter's future provides her with a rock-solid financial base from which to build up her own resources. If you save this amount of money each and every month until she reaches age 18 and then she continues to invest the lump sum, even if she doesn't add $1 more of her own, at a retirement age of sixty-five years, she will have a plump and mighty nest egg. She will have become a financially strong and independent woman. Read on!

The following figures have been brought to you courtesy of Tom Linzmeier, a stockbroker with over eighteen years experience and excellent money management techniques. He is also the author of *Making Your Living from the Stock Market: America's Greatest Franchise* (Little Canada, Minn.: Blue Walrus, Inc., 1994).

These figures have been tabulated for two separate savings programs, one extending eighteen years and one extending ten years. The first is if you begin saving the month she is born and continue monthly for eighteen years, at which point the saving can stop. The second is if you begin saving monthly when she turns eight years old and continue saving monthly until she is eighteen years old, at which point the saving can stop. Each of the two time frames have been broken down into saving the amounts of $25, $50, and $100 monthly. The original savings to age eighteen has been figured at 8% interest. The investing from age eighteen to age sixty-five has been figured at both 8% and 10%. All figures are pretax dollars. It is important to realize that the average rate of return for Blue Chip stocks over the past sixty years has been 10%, so the figures below are most likely conservative:

Saving $100 a month for 18 years at 8% yields: $46,565.21
Investing that lump sum for 47 years at 8% yields: $1,733,716.47
Investing that lump sum for 47 years at 10% yields: $4,106,934.42
    (Yes, you read right!)

Saving $50 a month for 18 years at 8% yields: $23,282.60
Investing that lump sum for 47 years at 8% yields: $866,858.05
Investing that lump sum for 47 years at 10% yields: $2,053,466.77
    (No kidding)

Saving $25 a month for 18 years at 8% yields: $11,641.30
Investing that lump sum for 47 years at 8% yield: $433,429.02
Investing that lump sum for 47 years at 10% yields: $1,026,733.39
    (Not bad)

Now if your daughter is already on her way, say eight years old, not to worry. You can begin saving today!

Saving $100 a month for 10 years at 8% yields: $18,012.43
Investing that lump sum for 47 years at 8% yields: $670,639.01
Investing that lump sum for 47 years at 10% yields: $1,588,651.03

Saving $50 a month for 10 years at 8% yields: $9,006.21
Investing that lump sum for 47 years at 8% yields: $335,319.32
Investing that lump sum for 47 years at 10% yields: $794,325.07

Saving $25 a month for 10 years at 8% yields: $4,503.11
Investing that lump sum for 47 years at 8% yields: $167,659.85
Investing that lump sum for 47 years at 10% yields: $397,162.98

If you don't have an investment broker, talk to your friends and co-workers. Get a referral to someone you can trust and talk candidly to. It's fun to sit around and dream about how big the numbers could get but without saving that money each month, no money will come back to you or your daughter. Money is simply a form of energy. As we put money-energy out, energy in the form of money will circle back to us. So, run, don't walk, to your broker today!

PLANNING FOR SUCCESS— ENTREPRENEURISM

The More She Owns Her Time, The More She Owns Her Life

Entrepreneurism is at the heart and soul of this book. It embraces the essence of raising strong daughters. It is vitally important to give your daughter an array of opportunities to develop inner strength and initiative. She will then have the ability to face the world with right-on certainty of her own identity.

Your daughter can be taught to be an entrepreneur. By this I do not mean only owning her own business, although that is an admiral goal. We will be looking at entrepreneurism in the larger sense of the word. The dictionary defines an entrepreneur as "The person who organizes, manages, and assumes the risks of a business." We will be examining the business of life.

Although I am a strong advocate of girls and women owning their own businesses, time, and careers, girls and woman can be entrepreneurs even if they hold "regular" jobs. Your daughter can be taught to always have other options and avenues for income bubbling. She can always be expanding her career identity so she is not tipped over by changes such as corporate restructuring, lay-offs, and economic instability.

Teaching your daughter to create her own identity in this world is no small feat. She must learn to make self-respecting choices about the type of work she wants to do. She must come to understand the link between necessity of creating work of her own and developing a lifestyle of her choice. She must realize that to pay for her car, her home, her clothes, her vacations, and her food, she must earn money. Because that connection is so undeniable, she would do well to begin thinking about what she likes to do early—now! Because she has to work to pay for life's necessities and luxuries, she might just as well enjoy what she does for a living.

I began easing into conversations about the work/living connection with my daughters when they were about five years old. I knew it was sinking in because as we were out and about one day, my then-eight-year-old saw someone doing work that did not appeal to her. She firmly and solemnly said; "Boy, I don't want to do that when I grow up." It lead to another casual conversation about what she does feel passionate and interested about. What would she like to do with her time and energy in exchange for money?

You can help your daughter find her niche. Realistically, her niche may change a million times between age five and twenty. That's okay. The idea is to get her thinking about the work/living connection. If she dreamily says she wants to be an artist, help nudge her thoughts forward with, "That's an interesting idea. I wonder how artists earn money? Where do you suppose they sell their artwork?" Help her think through how to parlay her talents and dollars into economic independence and security. Assisting her in expanding her knowledge and breaking through any limited thinking will burst open the doors and windows of opportunity for her. She will begin to form a natural path in her mind that links her interests and talents with the reality of creating an income. Encourage her to set up shop now. Earning money for any form of work done can begin her process toward lifelong financial independence and security.

We begin this section by talking about money. We are not talking about money-grubbing, "material girl" tactics. The fact is, the world is changing dramatically. The job market shifts and jobs abruptly end. Also, when relationships end often the money seems to disappear. Your daughter should never be given the message, subtly or overtly, that someone will be there to take care of her or that money grows on trees and will magically appear in her life. Let us begin to teach our girls what boys have been taught all along: to be financially responsible, secure, and able to support themselves and their families. Let's teach our daughters skills that will help them to never be financially dependent on anyone other than themselves!

LOOKING AHEAD—TOMORROW'S WOMEN

As we think about our daughters, we must always be looking ahead to the reality that tomorrow they will be grown women requiring strong financial power. Change is everywhere; it will affect every single girl both today and well on into the future. When she is a woman, change may be summarily dumped in her lap. Already, nothing is the same as it was even two decades ago. Then, safety usually came within the confines of a relationship, perhaps a part-time job, a role. Being a woman today is extremely exhilarating and sometimes painful. Today women can no longer accept pat answers from others about how to live their complicated lives. Yet, they are often negatively labeled if they don't listen to these other voices.

The women's issues battle has been waged tirelessly for years by women committed to making things better for their daughters. Unfortunately, rifts, divisions, and battle lines have been drawn between the working mother, the homemaker, and the young girl growing up. These rifts can heal when we acknowledge and accept that no one-size-fits-all answer exists for how women should live their lives. To continue to assert that only one, true answer exists for issues such as whether mothers should work or stay home and raise children is grossly unfair to women. To grant that all men (fathers or not) should be given the right to pursue any of a million different interests, but to assume that all women who happen to be mothers, should want to do only one thing with their lives (stay home with their children full-time) is ludicrous. If a woman chooses and is able to stay with children, that's fine. But realistically, how many women have that option? And is it a safe option?

A major concern is economics—specifically women's economics after a life-changing transition, such as divorce. Women need to have enough money to put food on the table for themselves and their kids (assuming they have custody). They need to have enough money to enjoy a bit of life—enough money not to dread holiday expenses or unexpected repairs or for opportunities missed because they carried a price-tag (and they all do).

Many of today's mothers, for a thousand different personal reasons, choose to either stay home full-time or cut back to a part-time career. They have an unwritten agreement for the majority of support to come from outside of themselves. The children are deemed important enough for someone to stay home, at least part of the time. Then, sometime down the road, due to changes from divorce, job loss, or a myriad of other life transitions, these women may find themselves in the uncomfortable situation of not being able to support themselves adequately. A recent newspaper article quoted a young woman doctor stating that it behooved all women with children to work only part time. Professional women with professional salaries can sometimes opt for that choice. In theory it is an attractive idea. In reality, most single parent women can barely eke out a family life on their full-time salary let alone a part-time one.

Ultimately, when the winds of change blow hard—from divorce, a floundering economy, a spouse laid-off, or financial setbacks, the preponderance of women find themselves unable to support themselves adequately. Unwritten agreements on division of responsibility leave them just as bright and well-educated, as they always were, yet financially stranded. Before, they had not seen the need to put constant energy into their career options. Many people still believe that children should not be subject to a mix of other priorities and

164

careers. This almost makes the statement that supporting herself and her children is a frivolous luxury. In fact, is it not one of the most basic human requirements that we be competent to care for ourselves and our young?

Times have changed. Women can no longer rely on relationships, wills, home equity, or savings accounts. Women cannot naively plan on having someone outside of themselves support them when their circumstances change. Circumstances change even after babies come. After a loss, trying to make ends meet can eat their retirement and savings accounts alive. If women cannot support themselves, reality can imprison them from creatively responding to life. Women may get stuck in low-paying jobs that neither fit nor interest them and certainly do not energize or challenge them.

Women can no longer even rely on jobs to protect them. Of course, not all women are suited for starting their own businesses nor are they entrepreneurial at heart. It is important, however, to plant the seed of self-sufficiency, no matter how small or grand. Stay-home moms, women working low-income jobs, and professional women can challenge themselves to find someplace in their lives where they can begin to take control of their financial destinies and initiate some self-generated income. Finally, women who live a postponed or on-hold life take a great risk. Today's changes demand that women no longer casually rely on anyone outside themselves to support them solely. Statistics don't lie.

What to do? Start now while your daughter is young. Start somewhere, anywhere. Help your daughter put some action on any one of her ideas. What a great time to experiment with things that interest her—now, before she is responsible for an entire household. Help her create some sort of work or investment that is hers, powered solely by her. Once she tastes the empowering sweetness of creating her own work for profit, she will be hungry for more.

When change knocks at your daughter's door, help her be ready to speak her own truth and express who she is through her work. Show your daughter how to depend on herself creatively. Wishing her happy fulfillment of her dreams isn't enough. Challenge her.

Teach her. Love her enough to show her how to take care of herself in this ever-changing, wonderfully challenging world.

SETTING UP SHOP NOW

Now is the perfect time for your daughter to try her ideas on for size. Challenge her to go ahead and set up shop now. The overhead is low, the risks are small and the opportunities to explore are endless. She could write a newsletter, sell her handmade projects, start a cleaning or lawn service, or do anything her heart desires. Teach her that it is never too early to act on her dreams. Whether her business soars, skids, or never gets off the ground, it will be an excellent opportunity for her to learn invaluable lessons in supporting her ideas and herself.

"An Income of Her Own" is a corporation that is spreading a new message that rings out for all girls. It is the concept that in the future, girls can bypass the usual contortions women previously have experienced when trying to fit into the corporate culture, join the ranks, or fit into "the system." An Income of Her Own offers a breath of fresh air by proclaiming the message that girls and women can own a piece of the system. What a great idea! Girls can learn early on the how-to of business ownership. Theme camps, conferences, and hands-on materials are available to help girls contemplate and act on their dreams.

Even colleges are getting the drift. Classes are now available where the assignment is for students to start a business and turn a profit by the end of the semester. Their grade depends on it. Let's get moving! What about trying this at the high school and middle school level? Why not even try it out on elementary school girls? The stakes are lower and easier to manage; the project could be in the form of a game.

Anytime your daughter enters into a venture with a future goal she learns the logistics of bringing her dreams into reality. Show her how to get the information she requires to research her goal. What will be required in the way of time, money, space, and outside help? Who can she talk to who is already doing something akin to what she wants to do?

The more she owns her time, the more she owns her life. If you can teach your daughter by example and by allowing her to "set up shop now," you are providing her early learning experiences that will later help her find creative solutions to unemployment or job dissatisfaction. She will avoid dependency on others for her livelihood and economic security.

Exciting stories of young girls starting their own businesses abound. One is a group of girls in Duluth, Minnesota, who got together to provide something that they felt the magazines currently available for girls were missing. This group felt that girls were not being taken seriously enough. They now write and produce their own magazine, by, for, and about girls and the issues they are interested in. *New Moon* now enjoys a national readership and is hailed as a first-rate publication.

Six months to profitability

What seed ideas could you support your daughter with to help her set up shop now?

Listen to your daughter's ideas and take her seriously
This very first business can be very tiny-times, yet it will teach her crucial skills of entrepreneurship.

Help her pick a business idea that would be an expression of who she is
Perhaps she wants to start a babysitting or lawn care business. Then again, maybe she has an idea for a new product or a service.

Depending on her age, vary your level of support
How much help does she need to figure out what materials she needs, who she can contact, and—most important—where could

she market her product or service? Help her figure out and learn how to keep "the books" to track her profit and losses. This can be a very simple one-page log of hours worked, expenses (for example, lawn and leaf bags for her lawn service), and income earned. Let her design her marketing material, brochures, flyers, and ads. Coach her without taking over.

Encourage her to learn about kids in business
Subscribe to a newsletter. Help her connect with a mentor who is willing to spend some time with her, teaching her the basic ropes. Contact women business owners in businesses similar to the one your daughter is interested in. Support your daughter in setting up a mentoring relationship. Accompany her to a women's career organization and buy an hour or more of time for your daughter to speak with a consultant. An organization in Minneapolis-St. Paul called WomenVenture, for example, specializes in women starting their own businesses.

Does she need a very small business loan?
Decide whether or not you will provide such a loan. The more she can start her business at a grass roots level, the more profit and less liability she will have to factor in.

Planning, marketing and working
Encourage her to spend some time every week on her new business endeavor.

Have fun!
Business ownership, while tons of hard work, is fun for her to own! It's hers. She owns it. She directs it. She runs the show. She's the big cheese! What an esteem- and confidence-building idea!

WORK SHOULDN'T HURT

Years ago I bought a plaque that showed Snoopy snoozing on the lawn. The caption read; "Work is the crabgrass in the lawn of life." It seemed to be a pretty funny statement. On one level, it's absolutely true. On another level it's absolutely false. If your daughter ends up doing work she dislikes she will come to hate work itself. Such a negative connotation is attached to work, probably because so many people get stuck in ruts with jobs that they hate. They have virtually no control over their destiny or work day and are constantly told what to do. What a drag for anyone. What parent would wish such a prison sentence on their daughter? On the other hand if your daughter is taught to use work as a natural extension and expression of her talents and interests, work becomes an energizing and interesting way to spend her day.

Give your daughter the message that work can be fun and vitally interesting! It doesn't have to be something she dreads—having to drag herself to it after school or on weekends. Does she already detest her job at age sixteen or her choice of money-earning activities at age eight? If so, let's roll up our sleeves because heaven help any girl who is in a rut before even graduating from high school!

Information

First of all, help her see her negative feelings about her work or job simply as important information. What is it that she doesn't like? The work itself? The responsibility? The customers? Is there some small change she could make that would fix the problem? Use this information to help her sort out what she likes and dislikes about the world of work. These small fork-in-the-road decisions help lead her down the right road for her future. The negative feelings and experiences don't have to stay negative if they are channeled into an information-gathering "data base" for further decisions. Negative feelings about her work are energy drains; they should not be ignored. At this early stage in her career process, nothing is written in stone; the stakes are low enough to engage in some serious experimenting.

Picture-perfect work

Daydream with her about her interests and how she would like to spend her day. What does her work day look like? What kinds of things is she doing and what kind of schedule is she keeping? How does she see herself getting paid—every week, at the end of a big project, from many different sources, or from one? What kind of work personality does she have? Does she want to work alone or as part of a team? Does she want to be responsible for drumming up her own business or does she prefer to have work assigned to her? All these and hundreds more questions are part of the process of her identifying her work style and personality. It makes for great dinnertime conversation, especially if you join in and do some brainstorming about yourself! Ask her for feedback on how she sees your work personality. It's bound to lead to some all around joking and teasing!

Taking herself seriously

Sometimes girls and women don't take themselves very seriously. Girls have dreams, hopes, great ideas, and creative solutions. Girls need to band together to offer themselves and each other important support and assistance to make dreams come true. Women have always networked. Throughout history women have talked together over the back fence sharing recipes, have been room mothers at school, have offered their support, and have provided whatever was needed. These support systems still exist, but the world of women has expanded greatly and now includes the boardroom, the political arena, and any other avenue a girl or woman has chosen to pursue. Networking is more crucial than ever. Encourage your daughter to ask questions, brainstorm for ideas, ask for help on a project, and get support from adult women who have know-how in the area she is interested in. As she shares her dreams and goals with other girls and women, she will be taking herself seriously enough to accomplish the things that are important to her.

Avoid magical thinking

When your daughter is ready to launch into a project be sure she avoids falling into the trap of magical thinking. It is self-defeating to let her plow ahead on a project or idea that is obviously, without a doubt, doomed to fail. Working out the bugs of any project is always a necessity. Even if her idea is a good one, complete with solid planning, not everything will work out according to plan. Nothing ever does. Spend time with her using a solution-focused attitude. Troubleshoot ahead of time any obvious, potential, or predictable problems either one of you can forsee. For example, how will she handle her (housecleaning, lawn-mowing, snow-shoveling) business when she is out of town?

Her first business project experiences will hold unknowns and unpredictable snafus. Lessons will be learned in the thick of things. Making mistakes or even "failing" is not a bad experience—painful perhaps, but not bad. Help her to look objectively at what went wrong to find possible solutions for adjusting her business or doing it differently next time. If she is starting to falter, to feel overwhelmed, or to feel hopeless don't be judgmental or negative. Don't blame or say, "I told you so, you just wouldn't listen." That statement is a real balloon-popper. It's not as if she can't see that a problem exists. Instead, ask her if you can be of help. Don't just jump in and take over her project. Ask her where she could use some help. Let her know to what extent you are available. Last but not least, do not do her work for her. Support but don't rescue.

Bringing herself to work

Whether she works at the hamburger shop or runs her own pet exercise service, guide her in the process of always bringing her personality to work—the real girl, with all her talents, personality, style, and flaws. She doesn't have to leave her real self at home while she trudges off to work. That's part of the problem for people who hate work. They dislike it so intensely because either they can't be themselves, they think they can't, or they just plain refuse to. They fragment their lives into segments: the at-home-me, the at-work-me, the social-me. Point out to her that she doesn't have to wedge herself into a dry job description. She can help re-create her work to fit her. That's clearly the beauty of entrepreneurism. She can mold her work completely to fit her style.

Giving herself credit

Every undertaking—minute or monumental—that your daughter pours her energy into deserves credit. This teaches her to stop the presses long enough to pat herself on the back and give herself an opportunity to crow about her accomplishments. It's great for her to receive accolades from the outside world. Awards, prizes, and income are great incentives. But just as important are the internal rewards she gives herself—the ones where she praises herself and experiences the satisfaction that comes from work well done and work truly worth her while to do!

PINKY SWEAR

The latest in a long line of time-honored childhood vows of truth, pledges of honor, and promises is "Pinky Swear!" With "Pinky Swear" you make your vow, lock your little pinky fingers together, and solemnly repeat, "Pinky Swear." So what does this quirky little vow have to do with entrepreneurism? Everything! It's about commitment!

Teaching your daughter to pursue her dreams is the first step. Step two is helping her commit to excellence and to the steps needed to complete a project. When your daughter is inspired by watching an accomplished woman and dreams of her own success, you can begin the slow, painstaking process of teaching her the reality of commitment and what is really involved in the long haul of achieving a dream: the step-by-step road to success.

172

Kids are not necessarily born with stick-to-itiveness. Some are. Most aren't. This is a personality trait that can be cultivated and taught. Help her finish the books she starts, weed the garden she plants, practice with the sports team she joins. Help her make her decisions carefully; explain to her the ramifications involved. Help her understand that joining the dance performance group will mean missing any parties or events that come up during that practice time for a certain number of months. Then, you will need to stick to it too! Do not get wishy-washy, letting her slide from commitment to commitment leaving behind a trail of unfinished projects and broken promises. She will never learn to accomplish her dreams without homegrown commitment, taught early and rooted deeply. Success demands commitment. No finish, no prize. Pinky Swear!

PINK COLLAR GHETTOS, STICKY FLOORS, AND GLASS CEILINGS

Collars that choke, floors that ruin dreams, and ceilings that stifle dreams. What's a girl to do? Let's start when she's really young instilling in her the ideas and skills to leap beyond collars, floors, and ceilings. If Superman could leap tall buildings in one easy bound, why can't girls?

A girl who is unprepared for a competitive, sometimes fierce marketplace can get swallowed up in jobs she has to take because she needs work. Most people need to work for a living. If she has learned ahead of time (from day one to be exact) how to mold her talents and interests into work for pay, she can avoid some of the common pitfalls of boring and routine jobs. Not every woman is interested in starting her own business, but to have even a portion of her income come from self-employment instills independence.

Stuck to the floor in the pink collar ghetto

By definition the pink collar ghetto is bursting with young women who are trapped in low paying service jobs—jobs that most of them do only because they need the work. Teach your daughter to avoid that trap. Teach her the skills that allow her step by step to market her true interests and talents into income.

At least two issues are wrapped up in the sticky floor of the pink collar ghetto. One is the reality of the work itself. It is often a boring, hurry-hurry job where she is always being told what to do. These jobs contain no room for creativity. The powers that be decide and that's that. The second issue is money. These jobs are usually minimum wage. Urge her never to settle for boring, low-paying work. Notice it's almost always young, adult women who are in these pink collar jobs. Most men are trained to realize they can't possibly make a living to support themselves and a family on minimum wage. It's impossible to get ahead earning only minimum wage. One has no chance to save up for emergencies and unexpected expenses. If she doesn't begin to understand this early on, she will spend countless pay periods being told what to do, performing routine tasks.

Glass ceilings

Being employed by someone else is perfectly acceptable. Obviously, many career interests and categories are filled with jobs in which your daughter is an employee. But whether she is stuck in a low-paying job or whether she is a high level manager, challenge her to plan on moving beyond a dry job description to carve out a niche for herself that makes her special, interesting, and marketable. She may choose to combine a number of work opportunities to form a mosaic of interesting sources of income. She could plan on holding one or more part-time jobs. This way she would not be dependent on any one source for all her income. She could contract out part of her time to an employer and devote the rest of her time to self-employment. Constantly urge her to plan on how to avoid getting stuck or stalled by an employer. Teach her how to avoid sticky floors and glass ceilings. Discuss with her whether it's possible to move through a glass ceiling. Will she have to avoid this work situation all together?

Attitudes and first jobs

Chances are she will hold a job as she is growing up. Even at age ten she may be starting to do jobs around the neighborhood. Begin now to teach her how to improve her product or service. Even if she is a teen who works at the burger shop, brainstorm with her how she can excel in her position. What can she do to go beyond her job description?

What good ideas or improved service can she provide? What can she do with her own attitude to improve her working conditions and environment? Now is the perfect time to start teaching her the skills required to be a good entrepreneur. Attitude and people skills are paramount for entrepreneurs! Lazy, bad-attitude, chip-on-the-shoulder people need not apply to the world of entrepreneurs. She should never be phony, but she needs to understand and learn how crucial a welcoming smile and a can-do attitude are if she is going to be in charge of her financial future. Entrepreneurship is not only business acumen and skills, it's attitude. It's a combination package of personality, style, and people skills as well as a great product or idea.

Teach her now how to get along with her co-workers and the public. It doesn't matter if she is only ten years old and raking the neighbor's yard, or if she's sixteen and working at the corner superette. Teach her the skills of smoothing over a rough and conflicted situation with a customer. Help her problem-solve and think through a variety of ways to handle customer concerns. Show her the steps to being responsible and keeping her word. If she promises the lawn job will be done Saturday morning, she must learn the value of completing her contracted work on time! Customer satisfaction is important no matter what her age or service.

175

On the flip side of the same coin, teach her to stand up and be firm and clear about what she will and will not do. She need not be a doormat because she is young and possibly even self-employed. She need never take guff or abuse from a customer. If she works for an employer, she needs to report the abuse and let a manager intervene. If she's working for herself, she can terminate her contract with any customer who is not respectful or doesn't pay promptly.

The skills she develops with her early jobs are the gifts of lifelong learning. Skills developed early make adult life much smoother and easier. Teach her these skills now when the world won't come to an end if she gets dumped by a customer or fired by an employer. If it happens, it will be a hard and painful lesson and she will shed a few tears but what better time to learn the ins and outs of the work world?

All these first-job issues need not be lessons from the school of hard knocks. Help her pick out really fun first jobs. Show her how she can take what she is interested in and try her hand at it. Let her know that she can pick jobs where she will have a lot of fun. Go with her to check out a variety of environments. Does she want to work at the bowling alley or start her own window-washing service? Or both?

Be her guide her in her first jobs but let her learn her own lessons. Help her move away from spending all of her time sitting around; instill in her the enjoyment of turning her interests and talents into authentic income!

LIFELONG LEARNING

Parents are ultimately more responsible for their daughters' educations than school systems! Here is a pop quiz for you:

1) Name ALL your daughter's teachers and the subjects they teach.
2) Name the principal, President of the Parent-Teacher Organization, and District Superintendent.
3) How many hours have you spent at your daughter's school this academic year, volunteering, participating, or meeting?
4) What school project(s) is your daughter working on right now, this week?
5) What level is your daughter on in math and reading?
6) Who is your daughter's favorite author?
7) What is your daughter's level of computer skills?

Use this quiz to heighten your awareness of how vitally important your involvement is in your daughter's education. Your answers to these questions are crucial to your daughter's educational progress. As parents, we need to get tough on ourselves. We are all busy, pressured, and overwhelmed at times by our responsibilities. Cutting a huge piece of our time for our daughters' educations is a deep and major commitment, but one that is incredibly important.

Actively involved parents have their fingers on the pulse of their daughter's school experience. It requires rolling up your sleeves and becoming an active participant in your daughter's education. After all, through education she will be taught the process of thinking her way through life. It is important that you be a part of the process of her learning to think through questions, dilemmas, and challenges. She must learn to trust herself to find the answers. She must become a lifelong learner who knows that even if she does not know the answer now, she trusts herself to be able to figure it out! You must not allow her to roll over and play dead if a problem seems too large to handle. You must teach her how to solve problems, step by step.

Helping your daughter choose the more rugged roads of math, science, and foreign languages will provide her with a solid foundation for her future. In this chapter we will focus on how to enrich your daughter's educational process.

HONORING BOOKS
HER OWN COLLECTION

Investing in a bookcase or even just a bookshelf can be a source of inspiration for your daughter in her quest toward quality womanhood. It is easy to go to the library and show your daughter how to track down books that focus on girls and women. In addition, help her start her own library collection of girls' and women's literature: books by, for, and about women. Consider giving your daughter one book about girls or women on each of your family's gift-giving occasions. You can get a paperback book for just a few dollars. If she receives say five books a year, by the time she is eighteen she will have a virtual library bursting with books honoring and celebrating girls and women!

Fill her shelf with biographies of women so she can walk in the footsteps of women who have gone before her, lighting the way and making her world a better place. Buy her mysteries where a girl is the heroine, fighting fears and solving problems. Let her read about everyday girls just like herself who are experiencing the same issues your daughter may be struggling with. Bring home the classics. They are available in a variety of reading levels. After she has read a classic, discuss with her how the lives and roles of women have changed or have remained the same over time.

Give her a wide variety of books—books that cover a myriad of subjects and women. You don't need to agree with all the content in the book but it's another great opportunity to talk with your daughter about values and personal beliefs in the circle of your family. Expose her to material that is food for discussion. Branch out into topics that lend themselves to spirited debates. What a great opportunity to introduce your daughter to the world of imagination and possibilities for women. Give her the message that girls and women are out there, in the real or imagined world, doing important things, shaping the world, and being heard. Help her build bridges between women of the past and the woman she wants to become far into the future.

Be a book philanthropist

Many schools already have a program in place where you can donate a book in honor of your daughter's birthday. If so, consider contributing a book about girls or women to your daughter's school library or classroom in commemoration of her birthday. As the donor she could sign a special bookplate and paste it inside the book. If your school does not have such a program, consider initiating one at your daughter's school. She could also give a book to the library at your community center, school district education center, church, or apartment building library (yes, some apartment buildings have libraries. Yours doesn't? Start one!) Spread the word about girls and women!

Censorship

Censorship. That most dreaded word among the literary world. I have a wonderful button that says "I read banned books!" The debates rage on. Does pornography lead to violence against women and should it be banned? Is violence on the rise because of trashy material available at the bookstands? Should school districts be allowed to ban certain books from the school library? How much say should parents have in determining what books are included in the school curriculum? Each family will have to come to grips with these questions and resolve the dilemmas for themselves. Your daughter will have to grapple with these issues in the real world eventually. Hiding materials to protect your daughter is not going to make life go away. Age-appropriate monitoring of what your daughter is able to digest and should be exposed to is different than censorship in its pure form. As your daughter grows intellectually, allow her to read alternative literature; this will provide her with an opportunity to think about the world of women in a new light. It will push her down new avenues of women's identity in the world. Try not to run from controversy. Be gutsy and tackle these hard issues with your daughter. Help her decide what kinds of material she wants to expose herself to. What kind of woman does she want to become? What better place to hammer out her beliefs than in your own personal family library?

Budding authors

The more she reads the more she will consider the possibility of writing her own material. This does not have to be as pie-in-the-sky as it may sound. Your daughter has a surprising number of opportunities to present her written words to the world. Girls' magazines have contests. Many accept unsolicited manuscripts, short stories, poems, or opinion letters. *New Moon* magazine is a prime example of a wide open chance for your daughter to contribute her own material. Other opportunities include the free community newspapers that arrive at your doorstep each week, letters to the editor of your local newspaper, school newsletters, church bulletins, or newsletters from any organization your family belongs to.

Then again, she could start her very own newsletter! It's a piece of cake! Just put her thoughts and the thoughts of any other girls she would like to include into the computer, print out the material, photocopy it and send it to as many prospective subscribers as she would like. Providing she has access to a computer (if you don't have one of your own, try school, the library, or many of the full-service photocopying stores) it's an inexpensive and incredibly fun forum for her to express herself!

LEARNING CREATIVITY

The secret to creativity is that there is no secret. Creativity is not magic nor the product of a genius level IQ your daughter was born with or without. Creativity is not related to arts and crafts. It will not make your daughter smart, rich, or famous. It is certainly not a bunch of ideas she has that she never puts into action. Your daughter needs to breathe her own breath of life into her ideas to make them come alive and grow.

Creativity is something your daughter can learn and work at cultivating for the rest of her life. It is learning to see options: the doors and windows of opportunity. When well developed and nurtured, this skill will allow her to take a most ordinary existence and turn it into an extraordinary life. Teach her to use her imagination and combine it with practical and down-to-earth skills. Help her learn to listen to that quiet inner voice of intuition that will challenge her to walk her own path of truth.

Many of your daughter's ideas are stepping stones to the future. False starts are part of the creative process; from her experiences, she will grow in wisdom. If she is supported in pursuing her dreams, a natural and solid foundation will form beneath her.

With your support and gentle humor she will be able to move

forward with confidence. Be careful not to laugh at her mistakes or criticize her failures; these behaviors will only nip her creativity in the bud. When you allow her generous amounts of time to explore and incubate her ideas you give her the message that her dreams and ideas are valuable and worthy.

Help her to believe in her own innate creativity. Help her develop a creative philosophy of life and learn where to find the necessary support she needs to launch her creative ideas. Without support it will be nearly impossible to accomplish her dreams. Believing in her is one of the greatest gifts you can give her. If she believes in herself and thinks she is creative she will be. If she believes she is not creative she will not be able to tap into the creativity within her.

Change is everywhere and life will not hand your daughter any guarantees. So help her to have fun in finding creative solutions to life's challenges. This will provide her with a solid foundation when a crisis or disaster threatens to tip her over. Help her to look always for more than one answer to a problem. Show her how to generate many ideas instead of one. If she has only one idea and it fizzles out, she will be deflated. Teach her that it is okay to be dissatisfied, or to have a problem. Then teach her how to solve problems by reframing them as challenges just waiting for her energy and input. No quick road to creativity exists. Help her to move away from the "shoulds" and "musts" of life and bend a few rules in a positive, groundbreaking way. She will need help to learn how to work her ideas into reality. She will need encouragement when she has to stop and clean up after one of her creative messes. Creating is glorious fun and serious business all rolled together.

No particular virtue lies in doing everything the same old way it has always been done. Show her how to channel her youthful curiosity and adventure into tasting a variety of dishes from the smorgasbord of life. Show her how delightful it is to put her own personal twist on life!

MATH, SCIENCE, AND LANGUAGE— VITAL COMPONENTS TO SUCCESS

Arriving on the little girl scene, not all that long ago, were Barbie dolls who announced: "Math is tough." Mattel wisely bowed to the pressure of outraged women and withdrew the dolls from the market. To appreciate how really stupid that statement was, however, think of it in terms of telling little boys that math is hard, engineering and science are just too tough for them, leave it for someone else smarter, bigger, better. What a horrible message to give our girls: that using their brains is "tough." If a subject requires work, so much the better. The job of parents and teachers is to break down each and every subject in school and life into a manageable size for every girl. The offensive part about giving girls the "math is tough" message is not that math can't be tough in and of itself. That's not the issue. The offensive part is that it gives girls the overt and subliminal message that having to chew on a subject is negative. It is urgent that we give girls just the opposite message: that using her brain, chewing on a subject, breaking it down, mastering (or should we say MStering it?) is a what leads to success!

Each girl is an individual, with individual differences, capabilities, and intellectual powers. Not every girl is going to be a mathematician or scientist. But each and every girl can learn math and science to the best of her ability. Each girl can reach her own intellectual potential. No girl needs the message that something is just too tough for her to tackle, because it's just not true! She may only reach "level one," but adults need to help her reach that "level one" that she is capable of. On the other hand, it really is rather amazing how many girls get overlooked in their talent and abilities in math and science. If your daughter is exposed to foreign languages, math, and science and is coached diligently, she may in all likelihood excel! Girls are smart. Your daughter is smart—in her own individual level and way.

MATH, SCIENCE, AND FOREIGN LANGUAGE

Why the focus on these subjects? Because they broaden and stretch her mind. Math and science help her think in the abstract and analyze data. As she grows these subjects will give her added confidence in problem-solving, not only in math problems but also in life problems. She will have learned to crack the code of puzzles, to investigate, and to arrive at conclusions. As your daughter gets older she will need these skills to blaze trails into her unknown future. The geometry or the frog dissection per se may not be the exact knowledge she'll use for the rest of her life, but these classes help her develop the skills and competence to add to her repertoire—the confidence in taking risks and plowing through uncharted material. If she struggles with math or science, you may want to check into programs such as Kumon Math, an international business designed as an individualized program to help kids master the concepts of math with understanding and increased speed. Other types of programs such as Kumon can help your daughter experience the increased confidence to forge ahead and the self-esteem that goes along with being able to keep up with the rest of the class. It's worth the time and expense if it helps your daughter feel capable.

Foreign language speaks for itself. It opens her mind and mouth giving her the ability to converse with the rest of the world. It enables her to include other cultures and dimensions of life different from her own. It opens doors and windows of opportunity to involve herself with groups of people outside of her own familiar neighborhood. Wouldn't it be great if your daughter were able to travel world-wide feeling comfortable, were able to communicate in a variety of languages, and could handle herself in a diverse group of countries? Think what this would mean for her as an adult woman—the potential career and personal options this would open up to her.

Fun and games

The sciences require her to put her brain in full gear. Fortunately, you can do a lot of fun things as a family to help strengthen those brain pathways. Board games are a great way to have fun and learn at the same time. For instance, An Income Of Her Own[10] has a board game available to help your daughter by effectively introducing business and entrepreneurial concepts. What an intriguing blend of using her mind and having fun while simultaneously focusing on that all-important goal of entrepreneurism! Other games on the market can introduce and encourage your daughter to use her puzzle-solving skills. Include all the old, tried and true games such as Chinese Checkers (strategy), Monopoly (business concepts and property ownership), Mancala (math), Backgammon (strategy), Clue (problem-solving), parcheesi (strategy), Scrabble (vocabulary), poker (concentration, strategy), Memory or Concentration (both the name of the game and the skill) and for the younger set, Chutes and Ladders (dealing with setbacks). Your family can also set up its own games. Put some healthy competition in motion. If she's five, make a game out of finding and identifying as many different kinds of trees as you can on a Sunday afternoon outing. If she's ten, take a foreign language class together through community education. One night a week for six weeks will give her a flavor of another country. If she's fourteen, help her set up an extracurricular science experiment to enter in your school district's science fair. In all cases, you are supporting her and showing her how to enter into the world of math, science, and foreign language. It takes time. It take energy. Sometimes it takes a piece of your budget pie. It helps her grow strong and confident. That's what lifelong learning is all about.

Learning journals

One way to keep track of your daughter's academic progress is to

10. An Income Of Her Own, P.O. Box 8452, San Jose, CA 95155-8452, (428) 295-1097 or Jolene Godfrey (Co-founder) at (805) 646-1215.

have her keep a learning journal. Some schools are already doing this as part of the daily curriculum. It includes in-class written assignment, goals, interesting things learned, puzzlers to be chipped away at all week, and anything else your daughter deems important to her education. If your daughter's school does not include such a journal, start one at home. The contents would be different, but the goal the same. It's a place to keep track of what is actually being learned and/or accomplished during the week. Sit down with your daughter for ten minutes every Monday evening and go over goals, assignments, homework, and special projects for the week. It's important that she list her own goals and expectations for herself. Then make it a point to go over last week's learning journal, being sure to sign it and make a few comments of your own regarding her previous week's efforts. Perhaps even talk to her teacher(s) about starting a learning journal as part of the classroom agenda.

THE ARTS

When your daughter learns to understand and appreciate the arts, she is well on her way to becoming a well-rounded, tolerant, and well-versed young woman. Learning early to embrace artistic expression is a gift that will feed her very soul throughout her lifetime. Parents don't need to be great lovers of the opera or ballet or understand the modern artist to expose their daughter to a smorgasbord of cultural and artistic opportunities. For even brief moments, refocus your daughter's attention away from mindless television and onto artistic masterpieces. Learning to appreciate art is a skill that prepares her for a future of enjoyment. Opening hearts, minds, and souls to artistic expression creates a depth and compassion that translates into all areas of your daughter's life. When she learns to understand the meaning beneath a piece of art, she expands her mind and sensibilities.

Learning to take into her being a sense of artistic creativity keeps her from shriveling up and becoming narrow. Include in her learning process all forms of creative expression: art, music, drama, dance, and any other. The world is filled to bursting with beauty and elegance that she will never experience watching sit-coms on TV or trolling the malls for quick-fix entertainment. You do not need to spend every weekend attending cultural presentations. You and your daughter can sample and dabble to your hearts' content. Here are just a few of millions of basic ideas.

Read the classics

Read together as a family. Perhaps after dinner you could take just fifteen minutes to read aloud together. Pick a classic that she can understand, but one that can challenge and expand her thinking at the same time. Most of the classics can be purchased in simplified versions if your daughter is quite young. Start now. The classics can last your family at least from kindergarten through high school grad uation.

Attend plays

Some plays are expensive with obviously high quality visuals and well-trained performers. But an abundance of small companies put on family-priced plays with as much energy and budding talent as the biggies. The props might be hand-painted and the costumes acquired on a budget, but your daughter will be mesmerized by the story unfolding before her very eyes. Get there early. Sit in the front row. Read over the program to get the gist of the story ahead of time.

Visit museums

Don't just go to children's museums; go to real, genuine art museums. You don't have to spend hours and hours there. Just look at a few pieces if you would like or take a quick walking tour stopping to explore a piece that catches someone's interest. Point out the masterpieces. Stand around and discuss why that huge white canvas with the single red dot on it is considered art. What does your daughter think?

There are many types of museums. Historical, art, outdoor sculpture gardens, or theme museums. Check out the period rooms at whichever museums you go to. Your daughter will probably get into looking at the stuff people used to use and have a chance to see how her ancestors (rich or poor) used to live. Just relax and have a good time. There are no rules for the right way to go to a museum. Go however it fits your family. Just go!

Other performances

Get tickets for the opera, the ballet, and orchestra concerts. Read the paper and get on any and every cultural mailing list. You will find numerous offerings for the younger set. These productions are limited to one hour and have plenty of zippy music and creative onstage design. If your daughter is older, try to take her to one cultural event a month. Look around for traveling companies to expose her to touring groups from New York, Canada, China, South America, and Europe. It's a lot cheaper than going to these places in person! If she is taken to cultural events as a young girl, she will develop a lifelong interest and can offer far more interesting suggestions to friends than the standard, boring, "let's go to the mall" every Saturday night. Also, if you can afford it, bring along one of her friends. She will feel pleased to have a friend along and you will be spreading the artistic word.

Art Masterpiece programs

Be a volunteer for or suggest initiating an Art Masterpiece program at your daughter's school. Here a few artists and their works are presented by parents to their children's classrooms. The material is already in place; parents only have to study briefly some background information on the artist, present the artwork, and facilitate

188

a discussion about the works. It takes less than a half hour of time per parent, per artist. It teaches awareness and understanding of art.

Videos, movies, cassettes, and books about the lives of artists

A wide selection of material is available for in-home use about the life and times of various artists. Your daughter could be listening to a cassette tape about Beethoven (the artist, not the dog) while she plays in her room. She will learn about his life and hear his music in an entertaining and enjoyable format. Very easy listening.

Videos and movies are available about artists. Also, don't forget the wonderful classical operas and musicals that are available on videos. Check them out at the video store under the "musicals" section. They were made years and years ago, but the music and talent is unsurpassed. Don't be embarrassed to bring them home and announce that they are the evening's entertainment. Pop some popcorn and hit the VCR. Even old classic movies in general are great entertainment. Your daughter will fall in love with these old classics, even if they are in black and white. Don't underestimate your daughter's capacity to thrive on the classics. She may very well surprise you!

Sign your daughter up to participate

Sign her up for music lessons to play an instrument or sing. She doesn't have to be the world's greatest music lover or have any natural born talent to derive great benefits from learning to play an instrument or use her own voice. Or, encourage her to audition for a local play or just even take drama lessons. The lessons aren't free, but she can try out being an actress without the competition of an audition. Encourage her to participate in after-school craft classes where she can get her hands in the clay, the papier mâché, the paint, the art materials. An art class here and there can open up a whole new creative world for her.

189

Encourage her to enter artistic contests

Drawing, poetry, story writing, dance, or drama contests—she can enter any contest where she can try her hand at an artistic endeavor. It's not about winning first prize, it's about creating something from scratch and putting it out in the world for view. It teaches her courage and hones her artistic skills. Even submitting stories, articles, and poems to magazines, newspapers, and newsletters builds her confidence. No need for a competition for her to voice her creative opinion and talents.

As your daughter becomes well-versed in the arts she will grow into a woman able to form knowledgeable opinions and make thoughtful and intelligent conversation about art. She will develop a deep sensitivity to the powerful statements made by artists and will nurture her own aesthetic needs. This is no small matter in a world that has become increasingly harsh and bitter. Art is not "soft" but it feeds the souls need for depth, quality, and beauty. Art can be disturbing but it always pushes us to become larger and better people. It provokes us to think and feel and experience life from an artistic point of view. This is good.

COMPUTER LITERACY, FAXES, COPIERS, AND MORE

Does your daughter know how to access the "Electronic Superhighway?" Has she even heard of such a thing? Why in the world should you or your daughter even care? Because the world is moving at "warp speed" and she will need to know how to plug into the information she needs as she merges into the world of education and career.

The future is already here. Those of you who buy computers and such for your personal use are aware—you probably opted to purchase a computer with expandable space to upgrade. Perhaps it already is fitted with CD ROM, phone and fax modems and inter-active, virtual reality systems. Your fax may already be obsolete; your phone system introduces new features every few months including video options for conferencing. You can now use your computer to ask a question of just about anyone worldwide who happens to be online and interested in your question. You can communicate instantly with people on the other side of the world by flipping on your computer. It's exciting. It's exhausting. It costs money. Where does your daughter fit in to all this?

Certainly not every family is into electronic toys. They are expensive and not everyone feels the need to use the various services they provide. But when you introduce your daughter to them and give her hands-on opportunities she learns important basic skills. This enables her to move with ease and confidence in a world that is becoming more and more becoming electronically instanta-neous.

These mechanical tools are not just for boys or "computer hack-ers" or grown-up high-tech industries. If your daughter does not have at the least, basic computer skills by the time she is out of school, she will be left in the dust. Many preschools are now begin-ning to put three-year-olds in front of computers. These kids are as comfortable using the computer as they are turning on the TV.

When you teach your daughter how to access electronic infor-mation, you put the vastness of the world at her fingertips. Saving up for a computer or budgeting for an online information service is a lofty goal, but one with endless rewards. Imagine your sixth grad-er communicating on computer screen with someone in Europe or the former Soviet Union. What a wild way to have a pen-pal. Think about your daughter being able to access the Library of Congress for her next school project. Play with the idea of her being able to answer a question coming in from someone living in Australia! What a rush of self-confidence for her!

If owning a computer is over budget for you right now, keep in touch with her school. Stay on top of what she is learning in com-puter lab. How many hours a week is she receiving instruction?

191

What programs is she learning? What computer systems is she familiar with? Also, numerous places are cropping up where the general public has low-cost access to using a computer on an hourly basis, faxing information, and making photocopies. These service centers provide you with an opportunity to be involved actively in your daughter's computer education without having to spend a fortune.

As you find resources, teach her how to access different types of computers. Let her operate the fax and copy machines. If she is old enough, have her budget some of her own money to use for these activities. Help her understand the connection between these powerful sources of information and the cost incurred to use them. (See chapter 8). She needs to understand that this fabulous source of powerful information doesn't come free!

11
FEELING GOOD ON
THE INSIDE

Does your daughter ever get into a complete snit over some tiny, perceived insult? Do you feel like you have to walk on eggshells because she tends to make a huge deal out of nothing? Do you get worried because she seems so moody and depressed but won't give you even the tiniest clue about what's wrong? How often have you felt like everything was going along smoothly and still your daughter gets shattered and upset over seemingly nothing? Where on earth do all these emotions of hers come from? Why is she so easily set off? Is it something you're doing wrong? Is everyone else's daughter this difficult to figure out? Is it just girls?

At least society still allows girls and women to have feelings. Unfortunately, these feelings are still often portrayed as silly, related to menstrual cycles, to be expected from a girl, and in short, basically ridiculous. The emotions of girls and woman still are viewed with rolled eyes as overreactions, bordering on hysteria. Women's anger is still thought of as a mild form of uncontrolled insanity.

Let's explore the emotional world of girls and the reality of their feelings. It's true that daughters can portray a bewildering variety of emotions—sometimes all within one short morning! When she was younger you could predict her response. For that matter it used to be you could diagnosis everything as "she's tired, she just needs a nap." You'd plunk her in her bed and let her sleep it off. She woke up a new girl, or at least one a lot closer to the little darling you remembered living with you earlier that day. When she's older, it's not so easy. She will seem to have changed overnight. She changes when she starts school. She changes big time around ages ten to twelve years. And the changes continue, often it seems wildly out of control. Let's help her identify, understand, and channel her natural born emotional life. She should not feel ashamed of or embarrassed about expressing her feelings. This chapter will focus on some of the common feelings and emotional struggles girls may have as they grow and change. Teach her to celebrate her internal emotional life. Let's stop rolling our societal eyes at girls and women for having the courage to experience and express their feelings.

Feelings are complicated and complex. Each girl will experience her feelings differently. Individual differences are never so pronounced as when we look at the interior emotional life of any one person. For you to help your daughter through the often rough waters of her emotional development you will need the patience of a saint, a good sense of humor, a wide latitude for personal expression, a firm foundation of discipline, good old-fashioned practical reality testing, and an incredible dose of unconditional love. To a large degree your daughter's personality and emotional make-up came as a package deal from day one. She came into this world a miniature version of who she will be the rest of her life. As a parent, you will need to work diligently to help her keep on top of her feelings, to identify them, to express them appropriately, and to puzzle out how to channel them into healthy outlets.

Growing a daughter with good self-awareness increases her skills in the all the other areas of her development. She will be more confident in handling the other interpersonal dimensions of her life. She will know when she is angry and how to handle that feeling and solve the conflict appropriately. She will be able to express love and affection without feeling dependent or having to glom onto others, especially boys, for her security. She will learn to handle the

194

vicissitudes of life with aplomb instead of a roller coaster ride of moods. She will avoid the trap of always being the one to say "I'm sorry" when there is a problem, or of always being the one to give in to what everyone else wants. She will know when she is approaching overload with life's stresses and will be able to nip the anxiety in the bud, before it becomes full blown panic. She will know when she is starting to feel lousy about how life is going, the decisions she is making, and the relationships and situations she finds herself in. She will catch the early warning signs and be able to avoid the pits of depression and hopelessness. Bottom line, she will know her inside self well, which gives her the distinct advantage of being clear, focused and infinitely comfortable with who she is. She will be able to make decisions that are healthy and wise for her based on her own personal credo. She need not wander about, aimlessly looking to others for her personal identity or what decision she should make.

Learning to understand her insides is a powerful step toward becoming a strong and stable woman. It's distressing, the number of grown-up women who don't really know who they are, what they want, or how to establish a sense of identity. They discover long after they have physically grown up and made lifelong decisions that they aren't really all that certain of who they really are. Now they feel trapped and frustrated that no one taught them to figure out what they really wanted out of life. Help your daughter to establish a strong familiarity with her innermost self. Teach her to be comfortable with her feelings and personality while she still has a lot of time to establish a strong sense of her "me!"

BON VIVANT!

Bon vivant! Live well, happy and fulfilled, full of inner energy and peace. Raising daughters to feel good inside is a goal that naturally leads to high self-esteem, confidence, personal strength, and happiness. Life certainly can have its unhappy moments. As a parent, you will need to help your growing daughter with these struggles. Viewing the hard times as growing and learning experiences will help your daughter put some perspective on the hard work.

An emotionally well-rounded girl will generally feel good about herself. She will be ready to take on life and handle the struggles and tough situations that come her way. As a parent, the greater amount of positive "reserves" you can build up in your daughter, the stronger and more capable she will be in avoiding or handling the harder, perhaps painful moments of life. What can you do as a parent to build up these resources?

Always listen to your daughter

If she feels listened to she will be able to quickly process, make decisions, and move through hard times. She will feel validated and understood. If she is left to think it through on her own, a small molehill can easily become a huge mountain. Don't rush her learning, but be there to listen.

Praise and compliment her without smothering her in overdone, empty words

Try to find positive statements about her that really have some truth and substance. Empty words will go in one ear and out the other and won't do much to solidify her good feelings about herself.

Hold her in the highest regard

Treat her well and with dignity. Don't talk down to her or over her head. Talk directly to her at her level, with a small challenge and a nudge upward. Respect all of her, her opinions, beliefs, values, personal tastes, and privacy.

Show her how much you enjoy her company

Take her with you as much as you can. Include her in your activities and quiet time. Ask her what she would like to do. Try some of her ideas on for size. Let her know it matters to you that she is around. Include her friends when you can.

Show your own emotions around her

This doesn't mean she has to put up with every feeling you experience, but let her see you laugh (a lot), cry, and feel the wide array of feelings all humans experience.

Try to make her life as pleasant as possible

Whenever you can, add something desirable to her life. Paint her room her favorite color, fix her favorite food, read to her, have her friends over.

Fill up her life with great learning experiences

Read the paper and scout out enriching life experiences. Honor traditions but always bring the fresh and new into her life, too.

Teach her to be an "idea person"

Teach her to be the one who always comes up with great, wild and wacky ideas. The more ideas she has the more material she will have to create for herself an interesting and fulfilling life.

Ask her lots of questions

What does she like? What does she think? How does she feel? Be interested in every aspect of her life. Let her know you care and will be there to share to joys and help her with her struggles.

Hug, cuddle, kiss, giggle, and chase her around the house

MEN WHO LOVE

Men who love. Men who commit. Men who care. This is one of the greatest gifts you can give your daughter. The love and good relationship between a girl and her father provide the cornerstone to her ability throughout her life to develop healthy and satisfying relationships with men. With her dad, a girl can be given the opportunity to be happy and comfortable around men, which will solidify within her the ability to appreciate a man's unique energy and maintain healthy boundaries and expectations. It will allow her the necessary freedom to work through any issues, questions, or dilemmas she has with boys and men. Share with your daughter what works well in a father/daughter relationship. Share the wisdom, humor, commitment, and a father's point of view. Without an opportunity to experience a relationship with a committed man, a deep wound occurs that takes years to heal. In addition, we need to help our daughters recognize all the good men out there who are willing to serve as father figures for our daughters: the uncles, grandfathers, stepdads, neighbors, teachers, and coaches that help a girl experience interacting with good men.

At a time in history of unprecedented male-bashing and yet, alternately, undeniable proof of a plethora of "disappearing dads," it may be difficult for your daughter to sort out her feelings and experiences with men. In a home with a committed, loving, and generous father, she has a tremendously increased opportunity to experience and integrate a healthy attitude toward men. Unfortunately, many young girls are not so lucky. For all girls—both those with incredibly wonderful dads and those left high and dry with the end of an adult relationship—the media and the general air in society frequently depict men as leaving something to be desired, to put it mildly.

Fathers play such a vital role in the healthy inward growth of a young girl. Every girl needs her dad, with all his imperfections, "strange" male behaviors and yet, infinite capacity to love her. Fathers who withdraw into their own worlds of work, hobbies, personality problems, or relationships leave their daughters with a void that takes years to heal. After all, most girls will grow up and attempt to enter into relationships with men. How will they be able to feel comfortable, at ease, and confident with these new men without having learned and experienced the basics day in and day out, year in and year out from a man who can give of himself—a man who is there, who doesn't leave when the going gets rough, who has the confidence and self-esteem to reach out and envelop his daughter with the security of his love? A man who is glad he picked his daughter's mother to be his partner.

This is not to say that unless your daughter has a great everyday dad she is doomed to failed adult relationships. It is, however, a wake-up call to all grown-ups in her life that she does need some healthy male energy around her to learn the power of a loving man. A dad who abuses or abandons or simply makes it next-to-impossible for her to get close to him is placing incredibly difficult roadblocks in her path. She will have to figure out from scratch how to do the "man thing" as an adolescent or adult woman. This does not bode well for her success. An adolescent girl searching for male love can get into a disturbing amount of trouble very quickly. She easily begins to confuse love and attention with sex. She begins to tolerate being treated poorly just to have a boyfriend. She doesn't know how to find good boys and men. She settles.

Girls who have had the opportunity to develop satisfying relationships with secure, loving men have an easier time avoiding abusive, dead-end relationships. Why? Because they have learned what real love and caring is like. They have learned to know it when they see it and to realize when it's missing. Having a neat father boosts her chances of choosing healthy, well-rounded men for later relationships.

Where to Start

What are a few things dads can do to deepen a relationship with their daughters?

Do tons of things together

Spend lots of time working, playing, or doing chores together. Whenever you can, bring your daughter along or have her join you. Do fun things together that she likes to do. Show her that men pay attention to her, what she likes, and what she wants.

Create special dad and daughter times

Perhaps one night or a Saturday afternoon a month could be set aside for just the two of you. Plan something special that your daughter would like to do. Whether she is three or sixteen, time with dad can be very special.

Take her along when you engage in your interests and hobbies

Take her fishing with you or to a ball game or to the hardware store. Take her when you get the car serviced or when you run errands. Let her participate in things you like to do as a man.

Read to her

Pick out a good book and sit down and read together. Also, you can read books aloud on cassette tapes for your daughter to listen to on her tape recorder to help her relax and go to sleep.

Do physical activities with her

Help her to get comfortable doing action-oriented activities around men and boys. So many girls feel silly around boys and men and won't get active.

Talk to her about men and boys

Give her some details about how girls and boys may see the world differently. Talk about how each gender brings into the world and into relationships a unique perspective.

Let her hear you talk about women in a positive, affirming way

Let her hear you praise women, especially her mother and her! But don't dwell on physical looks. Make esteem-building comments about how wonderful you think girls and women are.

Express your concerns about negative behaviors you see in some boys and men in this society

Discuss these subjects in earnest and assure her not all men do these negative things.

Stay with her to resolve any conflicts you two may get into

Help her negotiate and resolve conflict between you so she can learn how to tell men how she feels and how to problem-solve communication glitches, hurt feelings, and concerns.

Be yourself

Be the wonderful, unique man that you are. You will be giving your daughter an incredibly wonderful gift.

EXPECTING BOYS TO BE RESPECTFUL

After all these years it still amazes me how many girls sit in my office and describe boyfriends that hit them, call them disgusting names, tell them they have to stay with him because "who else would go out with you, you're so fat and ugly." These are girls from "good" families with parents who care, bring their daughters to counseling, stay on top of their daily activities, and are heartsick that their daughters are putting up with such garbage. If they only knew the half of it. These are girls who are bright and attractive yet sit around waiting for these guys to call. They claim they have no idea why they put up with it but say they can't leave them. Usually they are afraid of hurting his feelings!

No one can say exactly why any girl (or woman) tolerates this treatment. Most just want to be loved, given attention, and made to feel good about themselves. "Sometimes he tells me I look nice; he's really jealous if another guy talks to me." This to her is proof enough that she is lovable.

Even younger girls—elementary school age—can be subjected to disrespect by boys. It's usually thought of as joking, as a lot of laughter and snickering accompany their comments and actions. A parent's dilemma is discerning which comments are childhood teasing and knowing when the line gets crossed to where it should not be tolerated. Many little girls find ways to protect themselves early on. Many kindergarten girls refuse to wear dresses to school, not only because they prefer the comfort of slacks but because they fear the taunting they will receive if anything should accidentally show. The up side to slacks is the clear preference that girls are now demonstrating for being able to climb and turn upside down on the playground. The girls don't just stand around playing hopscotch and giggling in little clusters like they used to.

Educating boys

A huge chunk of what needs to happen is the education of little boys. Clear and strong messages need to be sent from all adults—but particularly their fathers—that disrespect of girls will not be tolerated. This also takes awareness on dad's part to make sure he is not inadvertently sending double messages to his son. Parents—dads in particular—need to examine how they treat girls and women. What kinds of off-hand remarks about women in the media, women drivers, women in politics, or women in general, come out of dad's mouth? Even "mild" forms of prejudice against women will leave their marks inside the minds of boys.

To break the vicious cycle of boys dominating girls, boys will need to learn other ways to feel powerful and good about themselves without dominating or tormenting girls. When males continue to relate to females in the same old tired and abusive ways, these behaviors make their way all the way into the corporate structure. They show themselves as the glass ceiling (more refined perhaps, but still the enactment of male dominance and superiority). Many women still have to fight their way through enormous obstacles to even come close to what the men have achieved.

How can you help your daughter become inwardly strong enough to blast through this ingrained prejudice? How can you support her early on to establish a foundation that has the potential to grow into a healthy, robust, and powerful sense of self-value?

Great dads

Having a good relationship with her dad is an important beginning. Reread the section on Men Who Love (pages 198-201). Dads play an enormous role in how girls expect to be treated. If they are still working hard trying to achieve their dads' love they may just transfer this search to boyfriends. Dads don't have to be perfect, or even come close. They just have to be capable of genuinely loving their daughters and expressing that love in a way that their daughters can see and experience. As girls grow older they will continue to relate to men in much the same fashion they relate to their dads.

No dad in sight? Your daughter can still grow up just fine. Try to be on the lookout for male teachers at her school; ask to have her placed in his class. Call on uncles, grandparents, coaches, or neighbors to get involved with your daughter. Give her opportunities to interact with healthy men who can show her that men can be supportive people who help build up (and never drag down) her inner confidence.

The myth of male authority

Teach your daughter that a man's opinion of her is not the be-all and end-all. What matters the most is what she thinks of herself. This is an obvious message, yet it is surprisingly difficult to convince many girls of it's truth. At some point along the way, many girls begin to hand over the final authority on themselves to men! They don't value their own inner voice enough to have it override outside opinion. The opinion of boys carries more weight. Parents will be fighting a societal battle with this one. The reality of girls wanting to win the favor of boys is not wrong per se. Most girls eventually will want to be in a relationship with a boy and later a man. What is disturbing is the turning over of personal power and self-esteem, the allowing of a boy to decide for her whether she's good enough. Discuss with her the importance of balancing the power of women and men. Show her the balance of power, negotiation, and compromise between mother and father, male and female relatives, co-workers, and friends. Show her genuine respect of all women, whether you agree with the woman or not. Correct her each and every time she makes snide remarks about herself. When you hear comments, see movies, or hear about media stories where girls or women are viewed as less important than boys or men, Stop! Make the correction right then and there. Emphatically state the truth and make it abundantly clear that in your family, that is not so. Society continues to tolerate the diminishing of women. Each family needs to be in charge of changing that belief for themselves, in their families, in their households. It is certainly effective to make corrections within the structure of your family. Insist that your sons be respectful of their sister and mother. Show them a father who is committed to pushing against the river of society—a man who is willing to put forth enormous effort to change within his family the long-standing trend of women being treated as second-class citizens.

Families where girls are being physically, sexually, or verbally abused often put forth an unspoken rule that boys are more valuable and important than girls: rules that quiet girls and give power to males; rules that put the needs and wants of boys and men first even at the expense of girls; rules that praise and admire boys and neglect and ignore girls. These girls are guaranteed to grow up with a skewed sense of who is valuable and worthwhile. These girls do not develop the deep personal self-regard and dignity that is required of them to grow up strong and confident. Not having learned any other way, they will always defer to boys and men. They will always relinquish personal power to those they hold as superior: males. Make sure your family does not strip your daughter of her personal rights and power. Never cross boundaries that abuse or denigrate a girl or woman. Teach her inner dignity by treating her with the respect she so richly deserves. Your daughter can then be free to grow into a self-respecting woman!

FEAR BUSTERS
WHAT TO DO WHEN SHE DOESN'T FEEL CONFIDENT

Most girls experience a variety of often unnameable fears during their growing up process. Some large and overwhelming and some small, almost nuisance-like fears. Your daughter's fears will impact the entire family, eating away at time and energy and sometimes frustrating parents and teachers who are at a loss as to what to do to quell these fears in a normally confident girl. Even girls who are seen as risk-takers and leaders at school can suffer from vague fears that control their lives at home. Fears can manifest around a variety of issues, for example, being left alone, eating/weight-gain/body-image, not being liked or included, or having something "bad" happen to themselves or loved ones.

When your daughter deepens her sense of personal value she adds a strong and important cornerstone to her increased confidence over fears. But you can do more things to provide the nuts and bolts to her feeling more in charge of her life, which will in turn put to rest her fears. Help her to be flexible and open to change and the unexpected; this allows her to be able to go with the flow rather than get caught up in fears. Uncertainty is a fact of life. The more she can adapt the better. Teach her how to find specific areas of her life over which she can hold control. For example, her chosen activities, her money, or how she keeps her room. Let her make decisions in these areas and let her grapple with the outcomes of her

RAISING STRONG DAUGHTERS

choices. Also provide for her a structure that remains predictable: family rules and traditions that she can rely on. A sense of "this is how our family does it" gives her a springboard from which to manage her life. With her own personal choices and an underlying family structure in place she has a fighting chance to overcome fears.

Loosening the grip

What about when her fears grow beyond what she can handle? Your daughter may be fearful because for one reason or another she is not feeling as secure and in control of her life as she would like. Don't blame yourself. You may be doing nothing wrong. Rather than pulling your hair out, change the focus to solving the fear problem by empowering your daughter to feel confident enough to loosen her grip of panic. If you think about it, we all respond the same way. When we feel threatened we tighten our grip, emotionally and sometimes even physically. We worry, pace, get irritable, cry, procrastinate, think about the worst-case scenario, and generally make ourselves even more miserable. Your daughter may be using fear as a "coping mechanism" to help her get through the other bigger worries that may be looming in her mind. She may also be picking up any fears her parents may be experiencing. It's ironic, but if you are having a hard time letting go of your daughter—letting her live her own life separate from you—she may begin to fret about your personal safety. She will freak out if you are late getting home or are fifteen minutes late picking her up. Or, perhaps she doesn't feel quite able to cope with the rigors of school. She seems to be doing well, yet inside she doesn't feel comfortable. She feels like she's behind and running to keep up. So, when bedtime rolls around, she doesn't want to go to bed on time. She wants to extend the "safe" time of being home in a situation she feels comfortable in. And mornings aren't much better. Headaches, stomachaches, and unfinished homework are the start of every day.

These are signs that it is time to help your daughter feel more secure inside herself and loosen her grip of worries and fears that

206

she mistakenly believes will help keep her safe. If she is seriously ensnared in fearful behaviors you may want to consult a professional. If she seems to be exhibiting some normal fears you can try a few techniques to help her ease up and chill out.

Structure

First, provide the structure mentioned above. Assure her that you will be a solid foundation for her. You will be there for her and will listen and help her by empowering her but not rescuing her. Giving her a daily agenda to follow provides her a foundation. This can include bedtimes, bedtime rituals (even if she's fifteen years old she will probably have some "rituals" she likes to do—we all do), homework rules, guidelines for free time, and so on.

Give her areas of control

Second, put in place specific areas of her life that are totally under her control. A checkbook, Saturday mornings, choice of clothing, whatever you can live with and truly be able to keep your fingers out of. It helps calm her knowing she has specific areas that are completely under her control. She can do some things just the way she wants and needs to.

Push out the edges

Third, help her loosen her grip by pushing out the edges of her expectations. For example, if she is afraid to sleep alone, set a specific bedtime but assure her she doesn't have to go to sleep, she can just rest. She needs to find ways to comfort herself and be able to sleep alone, but you can agree to check on her every fifteen minutes, then twenty-five minutes, forty-five minutes, and so on. This isn't just for young girls, a surprising number of older girls get freaked out occasionally by the dark.

If she is fearful when you get home late, don't set yourself up for a specific time. Tell her you'll be home between 5:00 and 6:00. If she worries about getting sick, have her count how many days she has been well in the past month. Help her come up with a Plan B if she should get sick. Help her find options and ways out of her feared dilemma. Many girls fear getting sick. It's really a fear of loss of control. It may affect girls more frequently because often girls are not as comfortable in their bodies. They have not put their bodies to the test and found out for a fact that it will work just fine. They may fear aches and pains and feel weak and tired. They may cry in the mornings or when it is time to do something that requires increased energy to perform. These girls need a mega dose of security and self-confidence building. They require strong support and clear proof that they can cope and stay well and healthy.

Sleep

This is a good time to mention sleep. It's such an obvious need, but one that gets dragged out for so many families. Your daughter may require more sleep than she is getting. Too many parents wimp out at bedtime and don't firmly and matter-of-factly decide when that time is. Your daughter can certainly put in her two-cents but in the end it's up to the parent, not the girl, when bedtime is. She may not be the best judge. Observe her energy level, ask her teacher at each and every conference about her energy level and whether she seems sleepy in class. Without sleep she can't function up to her capabilities. Don't be wishy-washy. Don't whine that your daughter won't get to bed. Be in charge.

Never put your daughter down for her fears, no matter how absurd or irrational they may seem. Remember we all have our fears but a young girl may not know how to effectively combat hers. She simply finds herself caught up in her worries and at a loss to know what to do. Work with her to provide small daily stepping stones to self-confidence. This will allow her eventually to realize she really can handle this piece of life. Once she realizes she can figure out solutions to her dilemma she will simply let go of the fears because she will no longer need them!

ROTTEN MOODS

Everybody has bad days and rotten moods, including you, including your daughter. She may even be having a bad month. She feels like nothing is going her way. It may be particularly hard for her if changes are going on in her life: a new group of friends, a shift in her current group of friends, or a change in your family situation. Your daughter's life is constantly changing even though it appears stable and consistent. She may have new friends, new ideas, and new projects at school. Sometimes she gets overwhelmed, which can be followed closely by tears, irritable moods, and difficult behavior. She may just wake up one morning crabby as a tick, stomping around and growling at everybody. Nothing suits her fancy. The more pleasant and cheerful you attempt to be the snottier she acts. After a few valiant attempts to be the calm, understanding parent, you're glaring right back at her with a withering, slow-burn fury, miffed yourself and marveling that just last night she was in such a happy mood—laughing and apparently having a great time.

Girls today are under more stress than at any time in history. Life is not predictable. Roles are in flux. Everything is in opposites: the pressure is on to fit in, to be thin, to be liked, to have a boyfriend, to take drugs, not to take drugs, to have sex, not to have sex, to finish her homework, not to act smart, to be herself, to be like everyone else. The list goes on. If you think it's hard to figure out how to be grown-up these days, think how hard it is to be a kid, to be a girl.

Garden-variety bad moods

Sometimes she's just tired—overworked and underpaid with lousy benefits—the usual problems of being alive. When your daughter is in the middle of one of these short-term, garden-variety bad moods your support will model for her emotionally how to handle the bigger crises that come down the pike. These smaller everyday techniques will begin to give her the skills to handle the big stuff.

How to support

When she's suffering from a letdown, a rejection, or a perceived failure, be there for her in a supportive and practical way. Don't try to rush in and cheer her up right away. Let her vent her frustration, fear, anger, or hurt. She may walk around with it for a while, giving off clues that all is not right in her kingdom (queendom?). Go ahead and directly ask her if something is wrong. Tell her you notice she looks unhappy or worried. She may rebuff your attempts at first, but stay close without getting in her face. As she begins to talk (or vent), stay quiet. Don't interrupt or try to offer explanations—or worse yet—tell her ten different things she can do to solve the problem. Let her have her feelings. Show her you respect her feelings and troubles. You may not think it's much of a problem, but it's important to remember that young girls have limited life experience and don't have the skills to put problems in perspective. She experiences the problem as a big deal. Without diminishing her sense that this is big stuff, assure her that you will be there for her and will help her think of some possible solutions. Let her know you truly believe this problem is fixable and that you will be there to help. As she calms down and regains the ability to think more clearly resist the temptation to rush in with your vast wealth of life experience. If you do, she will think you don't understand. Why? Because your answers and solutions will seem almost "too big" and as overwhelming as the problem itself. Remember, solving this hurt or problem is not as easy for her as it might be for you. If it were, she would have solved it already!

Offer her tons of support. Reminisce a little (I repeat, *a little*) with her, telling her you remember how awful that kind of situation felt when it happens to you. Relate to her problem without hogging the conversation. Admit to her that you sometimes feel left-out, insulted, laughed at, or disappointed with yourself. Just don't go on and on. This is her problem time.

Alternatives to advice

Learn the skill of biting your tongue. The answer may be glaringly obvious to you, but then who's to say? Maybe it's not such a great solution for your daughter! Many clients come into my office for the first time hoping I will simply tell them what to do to solve the problem. They usually laugh a little and say they knew I wouldn't really do that, but it would have been nice. Actually, it wouldn't have been very nice at all. My solution might work well for me but be terrible for someone else. Every personality, every life is unique. We have no one-size-fits-all solution to any problem. Besides, no one has the right to tell others what they should do with their lives. The hardest part is realizing that we only have responsibility for ourselves and our own lives. Your daughter needs to learn that she cannot change anyone else. She can say what she thinks, feels, and needs but she can't make someone else change. A lot of people want bad situations to change from the outside. "If only so-and-so would do/act/be different, then everything would be better for me." Possibly. I don't dispute the fact. The problem is that no one can change anyone else. We're all stuck with each other, as we are.

Your advice to your daughter is well-intended but may not necessarily be workable for her. Even though she is your own daughter it's important to remember that you don't live inside her skin and mind. Keep in mind that the beauty of your daughter doing her own problem solving is her learning those skills for herself.

All the right questions

So what can you do? What works most elegantly is to learn to ask the right questions. Learn to talk out the next step. Ask her what she wants to do to solve the problem that is making her feel so bad. Help her move beyond "I don't know" or "I'm never going back to that school again ever!" You can help her come up with ideas just by directing the line of questions. You won't be telling her what to do when you ask her "How would you feel if you tried _____?" "What's the scariest part about telling your best friend how mad you are at her?" or "What are some things you might do to help bring up your grade on this special project?"

Personal responsibility

Without blaming her, help her own the solution to her mood. Put her in charge of her response. List how each solution she dreams up might work and what its drawbacks might be. Challenge her to think of at least three different ways to handle her problem and thereby change how she feels. Assure her that you will support her in whatever she chooses to try. Turn the responsibility for her behavior and mood back to her. Support her during her struggle but make it clear she is in charge of her response. Maybe she just needs to decide on a nap this afternoon, or agree to go to bed early and read tonight. Or maybe she needs to work up her courage and tell someone how she is feeling about something they did that made her feel bad. If she needs to chill out and calm down, help her figure out simple ways to do that to relieve her bad mood.

Sometimes it's easy to feel empathic toward your daughter's bad mood. You realize something painful happened to her today and you hurt to see her hurting. Then again sometimes you think she's overreacting and just having something akin to a temper-tantrum. You wish she lived across the street. In any case, you can gently but firmly make clear to her that she is responsible for her behavior and reactions. You will let her vent but she doesn't get to ruin everybody's Saturday because she woke up crabby or is struggling with a problem. When she's working hard to solve a problem, stick with her. If she's just off on a wild hair you may need to leave her alone for a while. Tell her she needs to get her act together a bit before you can really be of any help. She's not being punished; she's being given the tools of learning how to settle down. You don't have to try to reason or to problem-solve with her when she's off and running, basically out of control.

Tying up loose ends

When it's all over, later that day or in a few weeks, reconnect with your daughter about the issue. Sit down with her and ask her how she feels about how it all turned out. What solutions helped her feel better? Did she try anything that just made her feel worse? How does she feel about how she handled her problem? Her mood? How does she feel about how she acted? This debriefing session is very valuable. It teaches her the skills of reflecting back over her decisions, behaviors, feelings, and actions. She can learn an enormous amount from this type of reflective behavior. Show her how to handle her moods through a combination of support, limit-setting, creative listening, and question-asking. This provides her the building blocks that help her experience being able to handle her feelings in a way that she is proud of.

DEPRESSION—BEYOND THE BLUES

Depression is more than just a bad case of the blues. It's far more than a moody girl having a bad hair day. Clinical depression crosses the line from the common ordinary blahs into a state of mind that is much more difficult to overcome. Depression isn't something a girl just "snaps out of." The good news is that depression is treatable. The bad news is if it is left untreated it can lead to bigger problems and heartache for everyone. Yes, sometimes circumstantial depression does go away on it's own. This is depression caused by a one-time event, such as breaking up with a boyfriend, parental divorce, and so on. Time heals, situations smooth themselves out, and coping strategies begin to work. It is very difficult, however, for a young girl to manage depression alone. Remember, she does not have the coping skills or perspective of an adult. She does not see the "light at the end of the tunnel" that grown-ups can, because they have seen enough tough situations work themselves out in the long run. Also, depression can have a chemical and/or genetic factor. It can literally run in families. In this case, it may require medical intervention.

Parents often wonder how their daughter who has everything

going for her, is cute, funny, smart, well-liked, and a good student could possibly be depressed. What are they supposed to do?

The signs

First, be aware of the signs. The signs usually appear in a group, not one stray symptom here and there. This is a short list of typical symptoms. Your daughter may exhibit others or just a few from the list. Remember, everyone experiences some the symptoms on this list from time to time. Just be alert to your daughter sinking deeper into these behaviors over an extended period of time.

Feeling sad and depressed

She looks and acts unhappy. She makes remarks about feeling hopeless and sure that things will never get better. She thinks her life will never be fun again and has a dimmed view of the future. She believes she will never feel happy again.

Chronic irritability and moodiness

It's more than a bad mood and it doesn't to go away. She may snap everyone's head off and then she doesn't seem to feel any better after a good night's sleep. She complains about everything in a hopeless, defeated way.

Physical symptoms or fatigue

Some girls put their stress into their bodies. They struggle with stomachaches, headaches, fatigue, skin rashes, and the like. With depression, these symptoms become exaggerated and out of control. Tylenol and a nap doesn't cure these more intensified symptoms. She may also complain of fatigue and general tiredness. She sleeps way too much—more than the usual luxurious Saturday morning sleep-in. This is a girl who can hardly drag herself out of bed day in and day out. She wants to sleep rather than be with her girlfriends after school. She declines hanging out with friends and sleeps even when her siblings are out enjoying themselves. She

214

withdraws from social activities at school, at home, and with friends because she continually says she just doesn't feel well. A visit to the doctor comes up negative; symptoms do not match any physical diseases.

Weight fluctuation

She may uncharacteristically over- or undereat. All girls like to pig-out with friends here and there, but this is more. With this symptom she may hide the amount of food she is eating. She may be eating as a source of comfort, or she may decline joining the family for dinner saying she's just not hungry. Her weight may drop and she may develop an eating disorder that is primary or secondary to the depression. She considers herself fat and ugly and thinks she looks awful in everything she wears.

Loss of pleasure

Another symptom is the decrease in or loss of ability to experience pleasure. Here she has markedly lost interest in activities that formerly brought her joy and kept her interested. Nothing seems to pique her interest anymore.

"Bad" feelings

She struggles with a poor self-image and may feel worthless, guilty, ashamed, humiliated, or like a failure or a bad person. She may be overwhelmed with feeling bad about herself for real or perceived events that have happened. She assumes events are her fault and feels she should have done something differently. She feels therefore that she needs to punish herself because she can't live with the negative feelings inside. She may cry, complain, or be excessively irritable.

Drop in school performance

She just isn't interested in school anymore and puts in a very half-hearted attempt. Her school projects and homework are lukewarm, if they are done at all. She has trouble concentrating and keeping track of everything she is supposed to do. She may have been a great student but now sluffs off her workload. On the other hand, she may focus all of her attention on her schoolwork and ignore everything and everyone else in her life. If she's normally a good student she may feel school work is the one and only place left that she feels any real sense of control.

Suicidal thoughts or plans

This is clearly the most urgent sign. You must seek help immediately if this occurs. Contact a counselor or your family doctor. Don't wait around to see if she's just being dramatic. She may feel the need to pursue her lethal plans if she feels that no one is taking her seriously. If her suicidal talk is a cry for help, so be it—give her the help she is crying out for. Don't try to second-guess a young or adolescent girl. Remember, she does not have the life experience or perspective of an adult. She may just go ahead and try to harm herself. She does not have the cognitive abilities to really understand the finality of her intentions. Pay attention to any talk of plans to hurt or kill herself. Notice if she is giving away her prize stuff—her all-time favorite toys, knick-knacks, stuffed animals, or jewelry—things she considers her special treasures.

How to help your daughter

Take her seriously

Don't blow her off, laugh, tell her not to be ridiculous, or attempt overly to cheer her up. It is important to acknowledge and validate her feelings. Even though you may see the situation differently, that doesn't mean her feelings aren't real to her. Ignoring her feelings will only intensify them for her.

Be direct

Ask her what she is feeling, what she thinks is wrong. Let her tell you her story; don't interrupt. Tell her straight-out that you have noticed certain signs and symptoms and state specifically what you see. Directly express your concern and stay with her even if she

216

tries to shrug you off. Let her know you are aware and are not going to go away and leave her alone with her struggle.

Ask about suicide

You won't be putting ideas or notions into her head. She knows what it is and if she's thinking about it, she will be relieved to talk about it openly. Ask her exactly what her plan is. You can then nip it in the bud for starters as well as judge how lethal it is. If she is actively suicidal, remove all weapons from your home: guns, rifles, prescription medication, and so on. Don't get into an argument with her about whether or not she should live or die. This is not the time for a moral or religious debate. Don't talk in circles. Be clear. Don't wimp out and hope these thoughts of hers will go away. Take action. Seek professional help immediately.

Get help

Depression is treatable. For severe depression, medication may need to be prescribed. For less severe depression, counseling may be all she needs. Parents need to go to the counseling sessions with her. Make yourself totally available to the counseling process. The counselor will tell you if she/he wants to meet with your daughter alone. If so, wait in the waiting room in case you are needed. Don't just drop her off at the door and go shopping. A depressed girl is a family struggle; it is not just her burden to bear alone. She already feels lonely and alone. A counselor can help her sort out her feelings and get back on the road to good mental health, but she needs the love and attention of her family and friends. Be there. She needs you.

WHEN IT'S TIME TO SEEK PROFESSIONAL HELP

How do you know if your daughter and/or family need professional help? And how do you decide who to seek help from? Your family doctor? A counselor? The hospital?

Who's who

Your family doctor

Your family doctor or pediatrician is often an excellent place to start. She or he should be well versed in the common emotional problems of children and adolescents. It is often important for your daughter to get a thorough physical; many problems and disorders can have a physiological basis. If she is suffering from a weight problem, eating disorder, depression, or head- back- or stomachaches, it may not be just all in her head. A visit and an honest conversation with her doctor is a good place to start the process.

School counselors

A school counselor can be accessed through your daughter's teacher or principle. This counselor can help if your daughter is struggling academically as well as personally or socially. These counselors can work wonders if your daughter is having trouble with friendship or citizenship issues. They can help evaluate drug-related issues. Many of these counselors facilitate group meetings for students of divorcing families and those experiencing grief or loss and a variety of other topics.

Mental health counselors

I suggest you see only a counselor who has a Master's Degree or a Ph.D. in a specific mental health related field of study. I cannot stress this enough. You are placing your daughter and your family into this counselor's hands. Make absolutely certain this person is a licensed, credentialed professional. Most states license mental health counselors. Ask your counselor if she/he is licensed by your state. Be cautious! Anyone can hang out a "counselor" shingle and go to work on the minds and emotions of unsuspecting people who are hurting and frightened. Check your counselor out ahead of time. Make sure the clinic is licensed and that you are seeing a professionally degreed counselor. This is so important!

Hospitals

Hospitals are available for your daughter if she is in a life-threatening situation (for example, if she is suicidal, incapacitated by weight loss, severely depressed, or has any other conditions that meet the criteria of medical necessity).

Do we need counseling?

A family affair

If you decide your daughter does need counseling, remember it's a family affair. Don't plan on just shipping your daughter off to a counselor to "get fixed." Whatever is going on isn't just about your daughter. Parents need to be involved and are very much a part of the process. I am not saying it's all your fault. Good counseling is not about blaming. It's about putting heads and hearts together to work toward a positive, creative solution to whatever isn't working right. Good counseling—whatever it's theoretical orientation—is solution-focused. It is important to be there for your daughter to help her through this struggle.

Your daughter

If your daughter is struggling and the problem just isn't going away, it may be time to think about counseling. Counseling isn't a be-all and end-all solution to every little bump in life. Try a few home remedies first. Trust your own abilities to problem-solve. If the normal stresses of life get to be too much for your daughter she will begin to show signs and symptoms. Does she cry or get angry or irritable far more than any of her friends? Does she seem frightened and unable to cope with her fears? Is she withdrawing into her room, turning away from opportunities to be with friends and peers? Is she refusing to go to school, using one excuse after another? Is she complaining of feeling sick all the time? Is her teacher noticing that she is distracted or having difficulty concentrating, sitting still, or paying attention with the rest of the group? Is she being overly destructive of property? Is she running away from home? Using drugs or alcohol? Is she pregnant? A yes to any of these questions is a signal to you that your daughter and family might benefit from counseling. Counseling isn't magic, but if you work hard, you can bring about positive changes for all of you.

Counseling for you

Sometimes being a parent is painful. It can bring up shadows and shades of your own past. You remember all too well the painful moments of your own childhood: the loneliness, the fears, the anger, the rejection, the confusion. Maybe your parents weren't the greatest. Maybe they yelled a lot or hit you. Maybe they drank too much and made life miserable. Maybe they outright abused you physically, sexually, or emotionally. Chances are your relationship with them is still strained. You keep trying, hoping each time will be different, but it's not. You swore you would never treat your child the way you were treated, and now here you are, doing the same thing to your daughter and feeling just awful about it. It makes you cry and feel so ashamed.

You are not alone in your struggles with this. A good counselor isn't going to yell at you or shame you for your struggles with your daughter. You will begin to receive the help you need to get this burden off your shoulders so you can be free to parent your daughter with the love and happiness you dreamed you would have. If you didn't get the emotional support you needed as a child, it's next-to-impossible to conjure it up as a grown-up and have it available to pass on to your daughter. You need to heal your own wounds. It needn't take years of therapy where you dredge up every childhood memory; it can be short-term therapy focused on healing your own pain and finding new and healthy ways to relate to your daughter. It takes courage to make that first call. But, do it. Do it for your daughter. Do it for yourself. You will be glad you did. You will finally be free!

Mental health counseling

The counselor

A mental health counselor can be found by contacting your medical insurance company or by getting a referral from your doctor or a good friend who was helped by a counselor. You don't have to accept any counselor you have been assigned to. Make sure you feel comfortable talking to this person. Trust your inner sense about whether you believe this person can actually help you.

Here are some important questions to ask when meeting with a counselor for the first time:

1) What is her or his method of treatment?
2) What does the counselor identify as the problem? Do you agree?
3) Has the counselor worked with this issue before? Does the counselor think she/he can help?
4) How will the problem be treated? What type of therapy?
5) How long will it take?
6) What exactly will you and the counselor be working on together to bring about positive change? What are the goals?
7) How will you gauge progress? How will you know if things are improving?
8) How will you know when you're done?

Your part of the contract

The counselor can't do all the work. A lot of people mistakenly come to counseling thinking the counselor is going to tell them what to do and voilà, problem solved. Actually, it doesn't work that way. Even if the counselor fell into that trap and told you what to do, it might not be the right thing for you or your family anyway. The counselor can help you process your feelings, get some things off your chest and then come up with workable solutions that really will work. But (and here's the but), you have to be willing to do all the hard work at home, in between the counseling sessions. Otherwise, I can guarantee you that nothing will change. If you don't make changes, nothing in your situation will change. All is up to you!

Here are some helpful guidelines:

1) Be totally honest with your counselor. She or he has heard it all before and won't be shocked.
2) Ask yourself if you are willing to change. Not just your daughter or everyone else in the family. You.
3) Be willing to do any homework your counselor gives you. Read the book, attend a meeting, change your behavior, whatever. Be willing to do the hard work.
4) Be willing to reach out to your daughter. Do whatever it takes to help her through this. She may not appear very lovable right now, but now is when she needs your love more than ever. What you may have to do may be hard. It may require limit-setting and tough love.
5) Set limits. Don't be a doormat. Decide what you are willing to put up with and where you draw the line with your daughter's behavior. You are her parent and need not be slave to her demands.
6) Work with the counselor. Take responsibility for yourself.

Counseling is not magic but can help. Taken in the spirit of positive, creative change, your family can benefit greatly from rolling up its collective sleeves and working toward a better future.

12
HONORING FAMILY TRADITIONS AND IDENTITIES

We are all unbelievably busy; it's not easy to find time for the core-building activities we would like to do. Yet whenever you can incorporate traditions into your daughter's herstory she will be filled with a sense of belonging. Traditions that are lovingly enacted in your family are something for her to hold onto, something pleasurable she can put in her treasure box of memories. And when it comes time for her to make tough choices, she will be able to use the values and family bonds that she has internalized over the years to help make her decisions. She can call on the values she has gathered from your family traditions year after year to help make personally meaningful choices.

Will she remember family holidays as a joy or a nightmare endured? Will she have been given time-honored seasonal traditions to carry on that your family has enacted year after year?

Parents establish family traditions. Now is a good time to clean out the closets of your own family traditions. Which ones fit? Which ones need to be tossed? Which ones need to be stored away in the attic to bring out in the future when they will be more appreciated and understood? Make peace with your own family traditions and be in charge of the ones that you want to honor or discard.

Make time for bonding with *her*story and traditions; this will deepen your daughter's sense of values and connection to her heritage. She becomes part of a family that goes back generations and has come this far in its search for identity and meaning.

Exploring your family's traditions with your daughter will give her an opportunity to see how the "old ways" worked as well as learn to improvise and create something new. Have her join you whenever you participate in any type of traditional activities. These can include religious holidays, annual work around the house or yard, favorite hobbies, volunteering as a family, family talents, sports activities, food preparation (for example: canning, holiday meals, family gatherings), and personal interests such as antiquing, woodworking, sports, or camping. Let your imagination go wild. Think back to what your family used to do that makes you grin every time you remember those days. Look at your photo albums. What did you love to do back then? What do you remember your grandparents or parents doing that filled you with excitement and anticipation? Your daughter's joy is so easy. Her real joy is not attached to a price tag.

You can probably make a long list of traditional activities that your family has been doing forever. Share these with your daughter. Let your mind take you back to each holiday, season, and significant event. My mother always made gift enclosure tags for the Christmas gifts from the previous year's cards. Today, I still faithfully cut them out of old cards and run a satin ribbon through them. I have also made Christmas stockings for my daughters to match the one my mother made for me when I was a little girl. I still wrap up in a quilt from my childhood.

For those who feel their childhood was not pleasant to remember or had few traditions, this is an excellent time to create from scratch your own traditions. New traditions, molded into any shape you want, can also be passed on.

It does not matter what your background, heritage, or religious beliefs are. You can glean strength from your heritage and lovingly pass it on to your daughter. In years to come she will smile, cry or laugh at memories you help her create today to form the tapestry of her family heritage.

TRACING *HER*STORY

Tracing her heritage is an empowering and grounding process for your daughter. The "family tree" project at many schools has been laid to rest now that families come in all different shapes, colors, sizes, and configurations. The family tree idea is too simplistic for most families although the idea of tracing a life path is certainly as timely and valuable as ever. You and your daughter may find joy and surprise in tracing the path of generations. Perhaps she got to your family by adoption, a blended family, foster care, or a shift in the family structure. No matter how she arrived on the scene, she has a *her*story worth exploring. Diversity is such a key factor in honoring families and daughters. Society seems to be moving toward less rigidity about what is a family, despite backlash from some traditionalists. Piecing her life story together can provide her with a deep sense of security and continuity. She's not just an extra person; she belongs. Family structures vary but you can usually find a thread or two to begin pulling on—a portion of visible pathway leading to the yellow-brick-road of her past. She can spend years exploring. Her interest might heighten around holidays, birthdays, or family events. Then she may leave it alone for a while. Any connection she can make will feed her soul and leave her feeling satisfied with her work. She can begin tracking down her ancestors, ferreting out heirlooms, understanding her cultural heritage (both that of her biological family and the family she is living in), exploring traditions, investigating family "rules," beliefs, spirituality, and work.

Gathering *Her*story

All the important findings, documents, pictures, and letters can be kept in a journal or a box. Keep track of and organize them in some fashion; this will help her follow the journey and fit the puzzle pieces together to create the picture of her story.

Tracking down the relatives

This is really fun. It can mushroom into a local, national, and international project. (Note: If your daughter is adopted into your family, I would not presume to tell you what you should do with the issue of her biological parents. That is a private decision best left to you and your daughter. Whatever is comfortable for you and your family is the right thing to do. There is no one right way or right response for birth children or birth parents). So, as I speak of relatives, these can be biological relatives, adopted relatives, or even informal friends who over many year have become like family.

She can begin by asking questions of relatives with whom she is acquainted. Collect the stories and memories from everyone she can. Get names, towns, and addresses if possible of other less familiar relatives. Many of them may live overseas and may have children your daughter's age. It can feel particularly romantic for your daughter to become pen-pals with a long-lost relative of any age who lives abroad.

Most towns have libraries or cultural organizations that can help you track down relatives, living or dead. Venturing off to family towns to see the old places, churches, town records, cemeteries, and so on can be an educational vacation. Numerous books and cottage industries keep cropping up that help families trace their heritage. They provide workshops and creative ideas for how to preserve the stories, pictures, and heirlooms you gather along the way. They are also a wealth of information about how to track down relatives. The point is to provide your daughter with the unchangeable roots of her past. Introduce her to those that came before her. Hearing their stories is information to her about where her family has been and is food for thought about where she might want to travel with her life. Introduce her to her relatives—living ones, dead ones. They all lead to her.

Heirlooms

If you place even one small item in your daughter's room that belonged to someone in her past, that object will serve as a connection point between her life and the life of her family before her. Like traditions, they remind her of those around her who love her. Even an object from her own childhood can serve as a reminder of past happiness. Create a collage, a mural, a quilt, or a display. Show your daughter each item in your home that belonged to a family member. Attach a little story to it: who that person was, perhaps when the person acquired the object, and how it came to be in your hands. Your daughter may impatiently roll her eyes and make a beeline for the back door, but if told over and over, she won't forget. And someday, she too can torment her bored, young daughter with stories of the past. Not surprisingly, most kids get a kick out of hearing about their past and the favorite stories of yesteryear. She may laugh irreverently about fifty-year-old wedding and baby pictures, but they remain important nonetheless. Why? Because when woven together all the pictures, objets d'art, stories, and memories add up to become your daughter's story. Her life did not begin the day she was born. It began long before, providing roots and meaning to who she is today. Surround her with her past, the love, the concern, the plans, hopes, and dreams of everyone who walked before her. You needn't worry about the negative parts. As with all things, time heals. What she is left with will be the fragments and shadows of a time gone by. It cannot hurt, only support.

Investigating the family

Who were these funny-looking people with the straight faces and hilarious clothes, appearing to be having a particularly bad hair day in every picture? These are people who lived their lives in a different time and a different place. Who of them is living now and where are they? Who was the one who started that ridiculous tradition everyone goes along with every Thanksgiving? Learning about the

227

family will be enlightening and entertaining for your daughter. She will do well knowing the background of your family traditions, cultural events, and beliefs. Your family can be steeped in traditions, yet no one seems to know why or where they came from. Send your daughter on a mission to find out and report back. Why do you attend a particular church? How is it that certain foods are a part of your holiday tradition?

It can also be a good time to sort out family rules, figuring out where they came from and whether they are worth holding on to. Ask her what she feels is important in keeping a family bonded together and on track as a working/playing/loving group who are basically stuck with each other forever. That's as it should be. The circle of life.

ADOPTION—A WHOLE NEW WORLD

Daughters who come to your family through adoption have even more opportunities to be a part of *her*story. These girls can create a breathtaking mosaic of opportunities, traditions, food, and customs. Help your daughter trace the intricate path that lead her to your family; help her unfold her sense of identity step by step. As she builds bridges between cultures and families she joins hands with the people who have gone before her, linking her past and present while providing a foundation for her future.

Scout out opportunities for your daughter to explore her culture. Perhaps commemorate her birth parents on the day your daughter was born by planting flowers, making a contribution, or writing a letter. Feelings are often conflicted for adoptive parents; they may fear the possibility of losing a daughter to unknown birthparents. Birthparents struggle with this deeply painful and moving decision—it forever changes the lives of many people. They must remember and must say good-bye to their daughter over and over. Many quietly and privately send their love. We can take time to remind our adopted daughters of heritage, culture, and people with-

228

out fear of losing her. Helping her weave her native culture into the tapestry of her existence is a gift we owe her. We will not lose her by doing this. Besides, raising daughters is not about ownership, it is about commitment to love a girl enough to provide her with foundation, values, heritage, and family.

For multiracial families the opportunities to expand the entire family's horizons are endless. Many cultural and ethnic groups provide summer camps for kids, both daylong and overnight. This is a great way to immerse your daughter in a variety of cultural experiences, either her own or any other of her choice. The Concordia Language Villages in Minnesota draws kids from all over the United States for week- to monthlong camping experiences in many different cultures. Many ethnic groups also have organizations and newsletters available for anyone interested. Introduce your daughter to a potpourri of cultural experiences including customs, language, traditions, food, and values of your own cultural heritage, her birth culture, or any other culture; this enables her to learn how to interact with other people and cultures.

Many school districts now offer foreign language studies as early as preschool. Raising a multilingual daughter does not require that you fluently speak another language yourself. You don't need to know a word of Spanish or Korean or Chinese. Just enroll her in language classes in afternoon or Saturday community education classes. Be there for her as she studies. You can help her learn even if you don't know a single word yourself. Yet as you help her study you provide support and role-model how to be a lifelong learner. You are giving her the message that other parts of the world and her heritage in particular deserve respect.

Schools are also the place to help educate your daughter's peers in cultural differences. Many districts have introduced programs designed to heighten the awareness of cultural sensitivity. Becoming involved in this process allows you to have input into your daughter's education. Learn how the school is handling cultural diversity. Examine the curriculum being used to help children learn respect for people of other colors, values, and religions. If your daughter is of another nationality than you, she will need help in handling the questions, teasing, and stereotyping she will encounter. What should she do when she is called Chinese eyes? I learned after the fact that my youngest daughter when called "the one with Chinese eyes" stopped cold in her tracks, looked directly at the other child and announced; "I do not have Chinese eyes. And I am not Chinese, I'm Korean!" Yes! She didn't think there was anything wrong with Chinese eyes, it was just that that description was not accurate. We must teach our kids to be clear about their identities. We so easily take ours for granted. But, if we have foreign-born daughters, we cannot take theirs so lightly. Help your daughter form the sentences and gather the bravery needed to correct a teacher who, for example, says she has black hair, when in fact her hair is brown. When this happened to my older daughter, she sighed with disgust, "If they'd just pay attention and look, they could see it's not black. It's brown!" Not that there is a thing wrong with black. The issue is learning to pay attention and respect individual differences. This may seem so trite to those of us in the "majority." To those whose color and features makes them uniquely stand out, it makes a big difference!

You can also instill respect for your daughter's origin by learning even simple things about her country. Try spending a Saturday afternoon making a fancy dish from her birth country. It can be a hoot and also taste pretty good.

Families can also plan weekend forays or vacations around cultural heritage. Flying to your daughters' country of birth will probably not be a spur-of-the-moment decision, but planning as a family for a few years down the road can be the kind of goal that glues a family together. Everyone can help earn the money. Open a special savings account, name it something delightful, and go to work, all of you! Add your daughter's money to the pool and help her keep track of how much she is contributing. Let her know her $5.00 contribution is as valuable as your $100.00 contribution. Some families go so far as to take sabbaticals from their jobs and live and work in their daughter's birth country for a brief period of time. Not realistic for most, but a fun idea nonetheless.

Laying the groundwork for your daughter becoming an international world citizen can begin humbly at a very young age. Teaching your daughter to become culturally sensitive and knowledgeable is a smart thing to do! As you look into the eyes that perhaps look so different from your own, love blurs the differences, takes over, and glues us all together.

OF QUILTS AND GOWNS

Memories come in different dimensions, often pieced together from remnants of past moments. Remember special days and seasons gone by with your daughter by framing and quilting them.

Quilting

Tuck a storage box of your daughter's old clothes in the back of the closet. Give away the ones that are still in good shape, but keep the ones with stains and worn spots that no one would want anyway. You don't even need to keep the entire garment, just a good-sized chunk. Over time you will build up enough of a collection to make a memory quilt. Include old blankets, pajamas, or clothes she went to camp or painted in, her favorite pair of shorts and top, or a sock she decorated. After you have collected a few years' worth, make a quilt of priceless memories for your daughter (you may choose to hire a quilter rather than do it yourself). The quilt can be a small wall-hanging size or a large, cover-her-bed quilt. Whatever the size, it will be a source of memories that you can both keep forever. Each quilted square will serve as a gentle reminder of the picnics, birthdays, camping trips, and scuzzy blankets of years gone by. And when one quilt has been completed, start collecting for the next. Or, have one made for grandma and grandpa.

Framing

Do you have a once-in-a-lifetime outfit that your daughter wore when she was a baby? Perhaps it is her christening gown, the outfit she wore home from the hospital or airport (if she was adopted), her dress from her first birthday, or an ethnic costume. Dig it out and take it to a reputable cleaner. Then take it to a framer (preferably one who specializes in heirloom and antique framing), have it enclosed under glass, and have it framed. Then hang it over her bed. What a poignant connection to her past. You could also scrounge up your own baby gowns and frame your own link to the past.

You could also create shadow boxes of your daughter's baby items. Pick your treasures, bring them to the framer and enjoy reliving your daughter's *her*story.

SEASONAL TASKS AS HONORED TRADITIONS

If the roots of traditions are to be established, then the traditions need to be planted early and cultivated yearly. Don't lose out on this perfect opportunity to ingrain in your daughter a satisfying sense of important tasks to be accomplished. It doesn't matter if you live in an apartment or house, what religious beliefs you espouse, what part of the country you reside in or what age your daughter is. Each season of the year provides excellent opportunities to establish time-honored traditions.

Begin each season with a checklist of tasks to be done around the home as well as a list of fun activities that your family likes to do. Let her participate in each activity, be it work or fun. Living in the midwest affords me and my family a wide variety of yearly events, ranging from the fun of raking leaves and carving pumpkins to the sheer delight of getting the snowblower serviced. Whatever your task, take your daughter along. Teach her that maintaining her home, whatever it's size or shape, requires diligence. Teach her the value of keeping up with seasonal chores and adding a touch of pleasure to even the most boring of tasks. Repeat the events next year and the year after. Because each part of the country has such different weather and each family has its own set of holidays, not all of these ideas are going to fit for your family. Try on the ones that fit and discard the rest. Generate your own traditions. And above all, include your daughter in every single aspect of planning and participating in the events. Take pictures or home movies to record your progress from year to year.

Spring

Plant fresh flowers and vegetables
Plant one pot in the window or a grand full-scale garden, whatever fits your family. Have your daughter draw the plans and go along to pick out the blooms. Consider donating and planting a small tree or seedling in a location of your choice.

Clean house
Let her at her room, closet, and underside of her bed with a vengeance. Reward yourselves with a major treat for a job well done.

Let her help plan her summer vacation days
Order catalogs from camps, parks, and community centers. Decide whether to return to old favorites or try new ones. Is there perhaps one program she would like to attend again, forming the beginning of a tradition?

Service equipment
Take her along to service any outdoor equipment your family has, be it camping, lawn, or household. Show her what needs to be done. Spare no details. Put her to work, using her hands and head.

Holidays
Celebrate and decorate for spring holidays. Use baskets of flowers and bright, spring colors.

Summer

Participate!

Show her how to get out there and do fun things. Be lazy and crazy but don't just sit around and be bored out of your brains. Show her how to use this season to strengthen her physical skills.

Start a Fourth of July tradition

Put your heads together and figure out where to go, what to eat and what to do. Work as a family to put together a memorable holiday, to be repeated annually—rain or shine.

Fall

Chores, celebrations, and fun

Rake. Wash the windows. Clean the gutters. Pull up the dried garden plants. Winterize the car. Purchase or order bulbs for next year's garden or window box. Get firewood. Carve pumpkins. Plan a wild and crazy Halloween party. Make pies. Can peaches. Watch football. Let her do all the work with you. When you're done, eat homemade chicken soup and play games.

Winter

Dream of spring life

Read the bulb catalogs and plan for next year's garden. This can be a huge backyard event, or a simple window sill of herbs and geraniums.

Get moving

Go sledding or hiking in your favorite park. End the afternoon with sinfully rich hot chocolate or a strawberry float.

Holidays

Celebrate your holidays in depth. Find one or two new things to try each year and repeat a few of the things you have been doing for the past few years. Make connections to her past and the heritage of her family.

Celebrate the turn of the season
Acknowledge the winter solstice and brainstorm with your daughter how your family can honor this turning point of the year.

Take a winter vacation
It can be an overnight stay at an inexpensive motel or a grand two-week trip abroad. Make it your own. Include her in all aspects of the planning.

BREAKING THE CHAINS THAT BIND

In your quest for family closeness it might be time to reassess the family traditions, gatherings, and events your family has done year after year. Activities that felt magical to you as child may no longer fit into the world as you live it today. Things your family did as you were growing up often hold special significance to you even as an adult. At the same time that you wish to maintain nostalgic connections to the past, you aren't required to wedge your present family into scenarios that cannot be recreated from your past. It's the old square peg in a round hole problem. It can be disappointing when your own children don't cooperate with your long-ago-and-far-away traditions. Then again, maybe it's time to take a long, hard, honest look at everything your family is trying to jam into your busily scheduled lives. Perhaps some of the reason that these old-time traditions worked is that families weren't so pressed for time and energy. Nowdays, just finding the extra hours to do creative traditions is half the battle.

Decide which traditions you want to introduce and teach your daughter with the hope that she will carry them on with pride. You may also need to decide which traditions don't do a lot more than pinch your toes like shoes that no longer fit. Which traditions are simply empty shells that your family would really be better off dropping? Some family traditions are really quite awful for everyone involved. Everyone will be secretly relieved to dump them. These are usually the ones that carry rather painful memories. Holidays, family gatherings, and annual events didn't always go as smoothly and rosy as we would like to remember. Pass on traditions to your daughter that really will create memories with genuine laughter and happiness.

Bonding, not binding

Spend some time reflecting and remembering the traditions, celebrations, family gatherings, and annual events from your own childhood. Be as honest as you can in your assessment of them. It's hard to have to admit that some of the traditions from your past actually pinch and bind more than help create a positive family bond. Some traditions really do nothing more than drain time and energy. Try to remember whether they were really a colossal bore or whether you were just a little squirrely and didn't want to sit around for them? If it's the former, maybe it's time to stop pretending and just let this tradition go. If it's the latter, you need to decide whether you want to at least expose your daughter to this tradition your family has been doing for years even if it doesn't thrill her young heart. It's okay to give her a nibble of tradition that she can participate in increasingly as she grows old enough to appreciate it.

In your reminiscing you may come across some family events that are actually too painful to even think about. It's time to honestly sort out the good from the bad. Was it the tradition itself that brought out the negative side of everyone? If so, dump it! Or, was it just a few family members years ago that ruined things for everyone? If so, you will need to decide if the whole tradition makes you feel lousy because of the memories, or if there is a part of it that you would like to continue with your own daughter, but do it "right" this time.

Parents have to be careful not to load too much onto the shoulders of any one holiday or tradition. That leaves too much room for disappointment. Your daughter may not react the way you did as a kid, or the way you want her to. Remember traditions are about bonding, not binding.

Picking and choosing

You and your family can sit down and decide together which traditions to continue. Or if you or your daughter hear about something new you would like to try, go for it!

The main idea is to focus as a family. No one person needs to take on the responsibility of being chief-in-charge of all family events. Work together as a team. Sit down with your daughter and go through the entire yearly calendar of events: all the gatherings, favorite seasonal activities, holidays, and traditions. Make a list of everything. Then, slowly and carefully discuss each event and whether you want to continue it. Decide to drop the things that no longer carry good memories, or those that feel like an overwhelming burden. We all want to try to do everything to make holidays and family times great fun. But in reality they are often more fun if they are simple and relatively easy to accomplish. This doesn't mean just because it takes a little effort you shouldn't do it. All traditions take a little time, effort, and energy. It's only a problem if the tradition ends up leaving everyone feeling exhausted, cranky, overworked, and at loose ends.

Look at your favorite magazines with your daughter and pick one or two things to try. But forget trying to recreate everything the magazine pictures. Maybe it's carving six pumpkins this year with wild and crazy patterns. Or maybe it's decorating spring baskets with yards of colorful netting and ribbons. Or perhaps it's working together to grow an herb garden, just like the one you saw in the gardening book. Do what comes naturally for you and what you have the time to do from start to finish without feeling like a crazy person—forget the rest. Drop the painful traditions that weren't all that pleasurable anyway—the ones that make you sigh at the thought of doing them one more time. It's okay to discard those that truly do not fit your family anymore.

Enjoy your holidays. Actively engage your daughter in choosing her memories. Let her plan, explore, suggest, and work to accomplish something rather grand and wonderful for her memory box.

THE ODYSSEY OF THE SPIRIT

Does your daughter ever stop and wonder where she fits into the grand scheme of things? Does she ever wonder if maybe when she's dreaming she's actually awake and when she's awake maybe she's dreaming? Does she ever wonder which is real? Does she have questions and wonderings about where she will go when she dies and will you be there too? Does God look like anything? Has she ever lived before and can she come back again next time? What does her spirit look like?

Your daughter will usually choose to ponder and ask these questions at the oddest times: when you're peeling potatoes or emptying the dishwasher. I'm not exactly sure why that is, but it seems to be so. Maybe you somehow seem available to her. These questions and wonderings go far beyond pat answers. Can you let your daughter work out some these issues over the years and not halt her searching with pat answers? Sometimes it's hard to let our daughters struggle on their own. We want them to believe what we believe or don't believe. We want to tell them the answers, especially if we're convinced that we're right. It takes a brave parent indeed to let a daughter search and find her own spiritual truth.

Whether a parent's belief system includes a higher power or not, daughters will ask questions, search, and ponder the enormity of the universe, the gift of life, and the reality of death. Can we guide but not dictate, support but not presume? Whatever our religious beliefs, it's tempting to think and believe that we have the corner on the market of defining God. We draw on religious documents, organizations, and past beliefs. Some draw on a wide variety of

238

sources, others stick to the straight and narrow to arrive at conclusions about the supernatural. What if she rejects your carefully thought out viewpoint and believes something different? Or, what if she wants to pursue a spiritual path and you really haven't given it much thought?

America was founded on the principles of religious freedom. In theory that lofty ideal is held sacred. In everyday reality, it's not so easy for most people to exhibit religious tolerance toward other people, religions, or beliefs, let alone toward a daughter. That's just too close to home for the comfort of most people. But, it is important to leave room in her life for spiritual development. Let her explore the vast universe of her inner spirit.

Let her sample a wide variety of faiths and their accompanying traditions. Knowledge of other religions and belief systems does not mean she has to embrace them, it means she will have an awareness and sensitivity to others. It can be very enlightening, educational, and growth-producing to visit many different religious meetings and services. Let her experience what religion and spirituality means to other people. Help her to experiment with her spirituality, ask questions, explore, and ponder. Let spirituality be a part of her ongoing life process, weaving together tradition and new frontiers.

LOVE NOTES
A family tradition

Make small, inexpensive, delightful surprises a family tradition. You and your daughter can express yourselves and your love for one another through the giving of little surprise gifts and services. Teach her while she is young to be thoughtful and playful in her gifting of others by encouraging her to give and by bestowing upon her these same little love notes.

Feeling special

Your daughter loves to be remembered in small ways. You can purchase small, inexpensive gifts to present her at unexpected moments. Hide them under her pillow, leave them in a pretty bag on her bed, or tuck them mysteriously inside one of her dresser drawers for her to find at a later time (perhaps in six months when she gets around to cleaning it out). Think of small things you know she would like; not just something that you would like. I remember a woman who, for Easter, gave her young children baskets of flowers instead of hiding a traditional basket filled with candy and trinkets like their friends. She was hurt and miffed when she overheard them telling others in a withering tone of voice that they got flowers instead of a basket. It's not that children should be grateful only for the gifts they like. In fact, it is important that they learn the gracious art of receiving gifts with thanks and gratitude at all times. The point here is that this woman really misjudged what young children would like and appreciate and gave a gift that was obviously something she herself would have liked to receive on Easter morning. The idea being presented here is to be thoughtful of some of the small things your daughters would enjoy receiving as a way to express your love.

The joys of giving and receiving

An important piece of this idea is to both give to your daughter and teach your daughter how to reciprocate. This activity is not to teach that every gift carries an expectation of a returned gift but to learn to carry in her conscious awareness the idea of giving to those she loves and appreciates. Encourage her to dream up fun surprises to give of herself and her talents. They can be spontaneous or scheduled, perhaps on a given day each month. Don't hound her, because then her giving will be forced and stilted. Teach her to be playful. Make it a family tradition for everyone to be involved. Praise her and acknowledge her thoughtfulness when she gives a gift or service to someone—family or friend.

Freebies

Gift-giving need not be about money. Teach your daughter through example how to think up fun, pleasurable little freebies to give to the ones she loves. Ideas? Leave a "coupon note" that can be exchanged for goods or services at a later time. Breakfast in bed is a lovely surprise for a young girl. Make her favorite morning menu and put a flower on the tray. This is something your daughter can do for you, too. I remember how touched and genuinely surprised I was the first time my daughters, at the ages of only six and three, brought me breakfast in bed. My oldest had thought it up all by herself with no prompting or suggestions from anyone.

It's fun and cozy to add finishing touches on outdoor events. Make cocoa for her with floating marshmallows after she's come in from ice skating or sledding. Or a frosty strawberry float after swimming. Tuck unexpected notes in her lunchbox. Fix her all-time favorite dinner for her or once a month let her plan the menu. Out of the blue and for no reason at all stage a surprise sleepover party, pizza party, or movie party for her, gathering together her favorite friends. Their presence alone is presents enough. If you have a garden, pick a few blooms for her room. If not, at a small expense you can place a vase of a few fresh stems on her dresser. Fresh flowers are a joy for anyone. Send a batch of cookies to camp for a treat. Pick up little free samples whenever you run across them. Your daughter will love the little odds and ends you bring home.

It's the little things

Show her you care by remembering to do the little things she keeps asking you to do for her. It can be a true act of kindness to finally sew the button on her favorite shirt so she can wear it again. Stop and pick up some new socks for her if all the ones she has have holes in them. Take a weekend to finally paint her room with the can of paint she picked out six months ago that is still waiting on the shelf in the basement. Hang the pictures on the wall as she has been begging you since last spring. Put up curtains for her. Pick up a pack of batteries for her personal use. Send her a letter or a card in the mail. (It's always a delightful surprise to receive something pleasant in the mailbox.) Take her out to eat, if that's not old hat at your house. Even pizza or spaghetti is considered haute cuisine to the young. Let her invite a friend along. Bring home a paperback book or magazine and leave it on her desk.

The list is endless. The more your family gets into the spirit, the more the ideas will flow. They can be wacky and crazy and tender and cozy. They will impart to your daughter the message that you think about her often. If the entire family gets in on the fun, your daughter will learn the art of making others feel special. She can extend this to teachers, friends, and relatives. Everyone likes being noticed, appreciated, and made to feel special. In teaching your daughter how to do this, you will be giving her a great, lifelong gift.

DINNERTIME

Gathering together to eat dinner as a family may seem like a rather quaint idea. Everyone is extremely busy, flying off in a million different directions. Practice times for extracurricular activities often start right at the dinner hour. Parents work late. The back door might as well be a revolving one. And yet, if you can, try to find time to honor this traditional ritual. It's such a great time to connect with your daughter—eating and talking together, laughing and sharing your day, nurturing your spirits as well as your bodies. Busy families may find it nearly impossible to gather together to eat dinner every single night of the week. But, if parents set family dinner as a high priority, everyone will begin to make an effort to arrange their schedules accordingly. Try to make it happen at your house at least five nights a week. What can you do to make it more attractive?

No fighting

Absolutely no arguing, bringing up painful subjects, whining, teasing, hitting, food fights, or tormenting one another should be allowed at the table. Even young girls can learn to keep their hands to themselves and find something pleasant to say. Parents too. Dinnertime is not the time to bring up worries about money or bills. Nor is it time to scare anyone with talk of a possible job loss or work conflict. Parents don't need to fight at the table, either. Nothing kills an appetite or an enjoyable dinner faster than grown-ups shouting or talking mean.

Great conversations

Bring up interesting, fascinating, even controversial subjects and throw them out for family discussion. Did you read something interesting in the paper today? What happened at school or work? Bring up timely issues, such as seasonal topics, political issues, news stories, and planning for future fun times.

Keep the conversation positive

This is not the time to demand an explanation for your daughter's, or anyone else's, screw-ups. Mistakes do not need to be discussed at the dinner table. At least at dinnertime follow the old adage "If you don't have something nice to say, don't say anything at all." This is not necessarily a good idea across the board, but at dinnertime, keep it merry and pleasurable.

Expand your daughter's horizons

Discuss ideas and plans for her future. Think about traveling, vacation, college, career ideas, entrepreneurship, and school. Build on her interests and let her have the floor to dream and use her imagination to improve her own future. Look at brochures while you're eating, discuss interesting projects she is involved in.

Talk about school

This is one of the all time best opportunities you will have to learn about what is happening in your daughter's daily life. Ask a lot of open-ended questions about projects, friends, and class topics. Ask about teachers, lunch, and special events being planned. If you listen closely, between the lines, you will get a glimpse of how the world looks through your daughter's eyes. This will help you to parent her. You will be aware of upcoming projects, personality conflicts, struggles, and triumphs in the classroom.

Have lots of company

How fun it is to have company over. Meet her friends and have yours over, too. Don't worry about a clean kitchen or a fancy linen table cloth. Just invite people over. It doesn't have to be expensive. Ask everyone to bring a dish to share. If your daughter is having a friend over, have her ask her friend to bring something for dessert. Teach and show your daughter that dinnertimes are social times and it's a wonderful time to welcome others into your home. If you're busy, simply ask the other girl's parent to bring her over and pick her up. Having company doesn't have to be a ton of extra work.

Plan fun meals

Take an afternoon and make preparing dinner a family affair. Cut, chop, sauté, mix, bake, and make a mess to your heart's content. Try new recipes. Be daring and try to prepare a meal from another country. Vary your dinner style. If you live where there is snow in the winter, drag out the grill for a midwinter picnic. Have your daughter run outside in the snow to flip the hamburgers while you make the chocolate malts and corn on the cob. Or plan an elegant, candlelight dinner where everyone dresses up just a bit. Or plan a dinner around the vegetables you and your daughter grew in the garden. Or decorate your eating area with streamers and balloons and have a party. The point, of course, is to make eating together a fun and happy experience.

Have quiet family dinnertimes

Also important is making family dinnertime a quiet, peaceful time for the family to sit down together and connect. Every dinnertime does not have to be a souped-up (nice pun?) circus with company bursting at the seams. Most of your dinnertimes are going to be at the end of plain and ordinary days. Even when it is just a common day, with no special dinner planned, eating together still provides your daughter with a strong foundation. Your family is telling her that she is important and that your family taking time to bond together at least once a day is important. She will come to appreciate the times spent together and will have a solid tradition to pass on to her own family someday.

Use the after-dinner time, too

Before everyone scatters (if there is time) take a few minutes to stay together. Stay at the table or collect in your most comfortable room. Read a book out loud. Whether she is five or fifteen, read together. Work a crossword puzzle from the daily paper. Put up a card table and work a jigsaw puzzle. Sit at the kitchen table and collectively write a letter to the editor.

Personal responsibility

Assign your daughter dinnertime tasks. If you cooked, she can help clean up. She can feed the pet or put away the leftovers. Work as a team. Include her in the responsibility as well as the joy of being together as a family.

Kindness to friends in need

If you have a friends who are going through a rough time right now, plan a whole dinner, bring the ingredients over to their place and cook them a dinner prepared with love and friendship. It can be fun and easy—homemade spaghetti and meatballs, garlic bread, and fresh green salad. Let your friends help or shoo them out of the kitchen. They will never forget your generosity and warmth and you will be teaching your daughter to be aware of the needs of others.

CONCLUSION
ENJOYING YOUR EXTRAORDINARY DAUGHTER

Above all, the moment is here to enjoy your wonderful, smart, creative, bright, and extraordinary daughter! Constantly instill in her positive demonstrations of your love and admiration of her. Show her proof that she is your most important priority and treasure. Point out to her all the things you think are grand about her.

The growing up years are busy. Whole years fly by and it is impossible to reach back and hold on to yesterday. We often take pictures and commemorate the firsts in our daughters' lives. The first step, the first birthday, the first day of school, the first camp, the first prize won, the first graduation. What slips by us completely unnoticed are the lasts. We don't realize at the time that this will be the last time we do this one small thing with our daughter. We don't realize the millions of miniature eras that pass, until one day we realize we no longer can pick her up and carry her or she no longer runs to the door to greet us. Her growing and changing is as it should be. But sometimes it is the realization of time passed that is so hard to accept. Living in the moment is the best chance you will ever have to communicate to your daughter the depth of your love. Live simply with your daughter, creating the kind of family that sits well in your soul.

Dare to parent

It takes guts to be a good parent. It also takes a heart of gold, lizard-thick skin, a loving soul the size of the Grand Canyon, a billion sets of eyes and ears, mind-reading powers, the ability to foresee the future and draw on the past, a phenomenal sense of humor, the humility to say "I'm sorry" and mean it, a bucket full of tears, super-human energy, and the wisdom of Solomon. And that's just for starters. In other words, one minute it ain't easy and the next it's a piece of cake. And you never know from one moment to the next which one it's going to be.

And so here we are. Parents of a girl(s). Is our job harder than that of parents of boys? I don't know. Probably not. Times have changed so dramatically that each gender has its struggles and triumphs. The exciting part about raising daughters is the brave new territory into which we can lead our daughters; then we must let them forge on ahead, carving out their own identities and niches in a whole new generation—a generation that will move ahead without us. Eventually, we must pass the torch. Aware of that inevitable future, let each parent make a commitment to send their daughter(s) out into that intriguing new world as prepared, whole, and strong as humanly and superhumanly possible. Don't let her down with wimpy, ineffectual parenting. Be tough as nails when you have to and buttery, velvety soft whenever you can. Don't let her be the parent, control your family, or be obnoxious. Do let her develop into a first-rate uppity, confident girl.

As a parent

1) Respectfully reflect back to her her own opinions so she can hear and see herself in your voice.

2) Let her see you admire strong and capable women. Never disparage a woman because she is successful and confident. Let her see that you genuinely respect and honor women.

3) Do everything in your power to keep her safe in this world.

Show her through your actions that you care about her well-being. Take extra time and spend extra money to help promote her safety. Admire her physical feats. Go to her games. Let her see you in the audience. Watch her 100th soccer game with the same devotion and rapt attention you showed when you clapped for her first somersault many years ago.

4) Participate in the world with her. Work and play by her side. Get involved together.

5) Treat her with courtesy. Speak to her in the polite manner you like to hear from her. Enjoy your conversations. Soon she will be grown and gone and the house will echo with a mighty silence where once you longed for a moment's peace and quiet.

6) Value her and she will begin to articulate her value and self-worth.

7) Cheer her financial endeavors. Applaud her earned income.

8) Throw open the floodgates of success. Acknowledge her dreams.

9) Crow out loud over her creative endeavors. Show off her projects to anyone who will listen. Treat your daughter as the most brilliant girl to ever walk the face of Mother Earth. Present her with the gifts of learning.

10) Build up her self-confidence and self-esteem. Help her feel great about herself on the inside.

11) While giving her wings to soar, keep her close to *her*story. Express to her your pleasure at having her in your family as clearly as you did the first moment you laid eyes on her. Show her your complete joy that she is your daughter.

12) Everyday let her see in your eyes the depth of your love for her. Let her see the joy you take in her life. Hug her. Kiss her. Laugh with abandon with her. Let her see you cry. Dance with her. Play with her. Work with her. Love her. And then love her some more.

AUTHOR'S NOTE

As I begin working on future projects I would welcome hearing from you about what kinds of things you have found work for you and your daughter. I am also interested in your thoughts and reactions to the material in this book. I look forward to hearing from you!

All the Best,

Jeanette S. Gadeberg
c/o Raising Strong Daughters
P.O. Box 24214
Edina, MN 55424